WINGS (1927),
showing a Spad XIII.

WINGS ON THE SCREEN

JUNGE ADLER (1944)
Young Eagles.

VON RICHTHOFEN AND BROWN (1971)
with John Phillip Law as the "Red Baron."

WINGS ON THE SCREEN

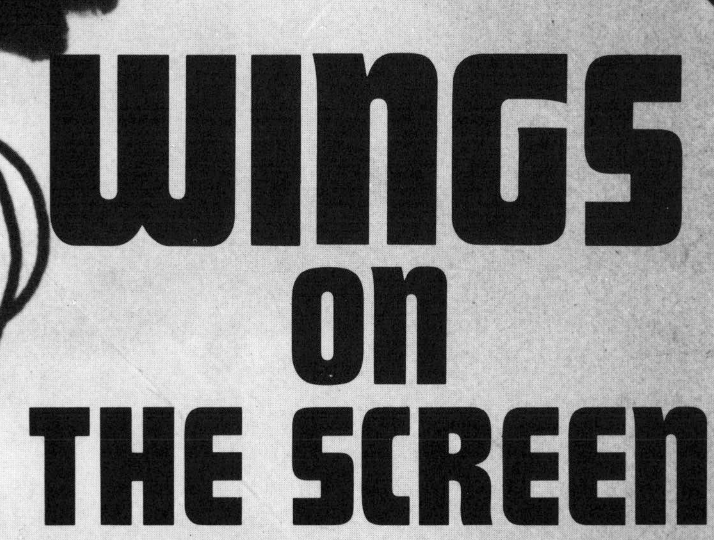

A Pictorial History of Air Movies

Bertil Skogsberg

Translated from the Swedish by

George Bisset

SAN DIEGO • NEW YORK
A. S. BARNES & COMPANY, INC.
IN LONDON:
THE TANTIVY PRESS

Published in Sweden by Bokförlaget Bra Böcker, Höganäs, 1981.

First American Edition
Manufactured in the United States of America

For information write to:
Jacket artist: Gunnar Jansson
A.S. Barnes & Company, Inc.
P.O. Box 3051
La Jolla, California 92038

The Tantivy Press
Magdalen House
136–148 Tooley Street
London, SE1 2TT, England

Library of Congress Cataloging in Publication Data

Skogsberg, Bertil.
Wings on the screen.

Translation of: På filmens vingar.
Bibliography: p.
Includes index.
1. Flight in motion pictures. I. Title.
II. Title: Air movies.
PN1995.9.F58S5713 1981 791.43'09'09356 81-4790
ISBN 0-498-02495-4 AACR2

1 2 3 4 5 6 7 8 9 84 83 82 81

X-15 (1961)

Who else has seen the unclimbed peaks?
The rainbow's secret?
The real reason birds sing?
Because I fly
I envy no man on earth.

Unknown American's flight poem

Contents

Foreword

Books about film have been written and often overwritten, but it seems to me that a book about aviation films will fill a gap and is long overdue.

It is with great expectations I look forward to the final product of Bertil Skogsberg's *Wings on the Screen*. The content—the variety of selected photos—all will bring back pleasant memories to me.

I feel privileged to have been part of some of these pictures.

Good luck, Mr. Skogsberg.

Glenn Ford

X US
V US
US

Introduction

Flying—the physical phenomenon by which a heavier-than-air object soars freely under its own power. This has always been, and continues to be, one of the most stimulating experiences known to man.

The ability to fly free as the birds, high above land and sea, was perhaps from the beginning of time the attribute most hotly desired by man. This ambition was finally fulfilled, but it took a long time to achieve; in fact, many thousands of years.

It was not until December 1903 that the Wright brothers, at Kitty Hawk, succeeded in launching a machine into the air that was powered by its own motor. Prior to this, Otto Lilienthal, a German, and John J. Montgomery, an American, had experimented more or less successfully with gliding; nor should we forget all the balloon voyagers who boldly ventured into the unknown sky during the eighteenth and nineteenth centuries.

However, although there are many who have claimed to be "first," it is still the year 1903 that remains in the history books as *the year flying was born*.

But from then until now, only seventy-eight years after those dramatic seconds at Kitty Hawk, development has been absolutely incredible. From the first small "flying string bags" consisting mostly of thin sticks, piano wire and fragile cloth fabric, the human brain has fostered steel monsters weighing many tons that can carry hundreds of people plus cargo around the world at twice the speed of sound, and at a height of fifteen kilometers.

And now *Homo sapiens* has reached the point where, in a wingless spaceship with tremendously powerful engines, he can fly out into the infinite distances of the universe and land on our nearest satellite—the moon.

To me this all seems fantastic, and it is not at all odd that film—a truly wonderful medium—has taken advantage of the possibilities offered by the poetic and exciting world of flying.

A great deal has also happened in the film world within the past seventy-eight years, but thousands of column inches have already been written about this and I do not intend to take up the subject here. The point of this film anthology is rather to attempt to say something about those films on flying that have been subjected to the arc-lights of projectors since the mid-twenties; to try to convey a little of the interest and pleasure I have enjoyed throughout my life in this particular genre of the illusionary world of the cinema.

Why then have I chosen to begin with the years 1927 and 1928? Many good films were made before then! True, but 1928 was the year that silent films passed into history and a new epoch in moving pictures began—sound film.

Since then a number of flying films have been made not only in Hollywood but also in Europe and other parts of the world. A study should of course include *everything;* unfortunately, this must remain a dream, impossible to realize.

In actual fact, there is an almost endless number of films that are associated with flying in one way or another. It has therefore been necessary to limit the selection. I have concentrated wholly on purely flying films; that is to say, films concerned with flying and the professional flyer, both in peace and war, in civilian clothes and in uniform.

Flight of Hawker Hurricanes (ANGELS ONE FIVE/1952).

CLARA
BOW

GARY COOPER
CHARLES ROGERS
RICHARD ARLEN

VINGARNA

(WINGS)

REGI: WILLIAM A. WELLMAN

En Paramount Film

My ambition has been to include as much as possible—with special emphasis, however, on those films which have made the deepest impression on me (and on others) in regard to the purely technical-aeronautical aspects, characterization, individual acting performances, political impact, and simple filmic qualifications. Although feature films predominate, documentary films have not been completely forgotten. There are a number of classics in this field, too.

With one or two exceptions, silent films have been excluded—largely because, during the early twenties, a film on flying was produced nearly every month. They dealt almost exclusively with the flying heroes of the First World War and were all rather similar and innocuous. Nothing *great* appeared in the genre before 1927 when the American film *WINGS* had its premiere—a film that was literally praised to the skies. It portrayed flying as a drama and was said to have exhibited a realism never before seen on film. Its success must be attributed primarily to its director, William A. Wellman, who during World War I had served as a fighter pilot on the Western Front. (See separate chapter on William A. Wellman.)

English-language movies have predominated in this special film genre and it is therefore natural that they occupy a dominant position in this survey. I have, however, attempted to describe examples of flying films produced outside the United States and United Kingdom, too. Thus Germany and Japan are represented, and I have included a few lines about flying as a subject in Swedish, French, Italian and Spanish films, as well as films made in Eastern Europe and the Soviet Union.

It has also been my intention to include as many illustrations as could be found. The catchphrase "at least one still from every film" has been adhered to, with only a couple of exceptions. (All titles appear in their original language, except Japanese and Russian ones which have been transcribed into English. All others will be found in the index.)

It is my hope that this flying film chronicle will provide a few pleasant hours, both for flying film enthusiasts and for others who share an interest in both films and flying.

In places the book may unfortunately read rather like a catalog, but this could not be avoided given the amount of material to be considered. It is on the whole not intended to be read through at a single sitting but to be used more as a reference work on a neglected film genre.

Contact! Release brakes! Prepare for takeoff! Full throttle! Glance through these pages and remember . . . !

KAHLE

When the Stars Got Wings

When Parisians were invited to something called the *Cinématographe* by the brothers Louis and Auguste Lumière in 1895, they could hardly have imagined that the thing they were about to see would rapidly develop into a worldwide entertainment. *Moving pictures* had come to stay, and during the first decades of the new century the live theaters suffered considerable competition and people were provided with a new interest and a new means of amusing themselves.

Through the medium of these jerky, often scratched but nevertheless fantastic pictures projected on walls, people were able to experience the world in an entirely new way. One could travel to distant lands, share new adventures, laugh oneself sick and be moved to tears. Film became a new medium of artistic expression and created a new profession—the film actor. Many of those who found a way to appear in front of the camera became stars, some big, others small. A few became legends in their own time.

The real artists of film—the directors—soon learned that with a little imagination the camera could be made to perform miracles. Adventure, romance, tragedy or comedy, everything could be presented, either separately or together, as a single dish as it were, suitable to charm the ever more demanding cinema audience. It was also important that film ideas should be realized at as little cost as possible. The producers and the smart ones, the investors, had also discovered the potential of film. Films cost money to make, but they also made profits—big profits. If this equation were to work it was essential that *good* films were made, films that could draw the public to the box office. They need not necessarily be works of art; success was in any case inevitable just as long as the public's need for illusion was met.

In 1928, the year silent film became merely a memory, the world had managed to pass through a war. Ten years had rolled by and the wounds from that period of horror had begun to heal. From this perspective, moviemakers discovered that war was the perfect film subject. In war films you could have everything—drama, excitement, tragedy, terror, love and hate.

War films had been made earlier, even films about flying. During World War I, flying had been a great adventure, cynically speaking, and had created real heroes.

In the early twenties, most flying films dealt with war planes tumbling through the clouds above the trenches, mud, and poison gas of Verdun and Lille. One or two pioneer airmail flyers were seen, too, usually with engines coughing and wings heavy with ice, drifting among the menacing peaks of the Andes. No masterpieces saw the light of day, however.

In 1921 a young man by the name of William A. Wellman arrived in Hollywood. He had a colorful past, among other things as a fighter pilot in the famous Lafayette Air Corps, consisting of volunteer flyers who fought for France against the Germans during World War I.

Wellman wanted to make films, but in the beginning he worked as an actor and spent the rest of his time flying. Finally he was given the opportunity to make films of his own, which were so good that he could soon regard himself as an established director.

Helen Chandler and John Garrick in THE SKY HAWK (1930).

Two of his earliest films were *The Man Who Won* (1923) and *You Never Know Women* (1926).

In 1926, Paramount asked him to make a film based on a story by John Monk Saunders, a former fighter pilot. It was about the war and dealt with a subject that Wellman knew—flying. Wellman approached the work eagerly and *WINGS* had its premiere in August 1927.

It was a great success with both audiences and critics and was considered so good that it was named the best film of the year and earned an Oscar in 1928 (the first, incidentally: the famous film award was established in that year).

WINGS was a pioneering work among films on flying. It was one of the last silent films, but it managed to show the horror and drama of war with a realism that totally captured the audience. The flying scenes were magnificent and very well photographed.

Briefly, the story is as follows: two young American friends, John Powell and Bruce Armstrong, played by Charles Rogers and Richard Arlen, go to Europe to volunteer as fighter pilots on the Western Front.

They are both in love with the same girl, Sylvia Lewis (Jobyna Ralston), but only Armstrong gets any response to his feelings. Through a misunderstanding, Powell believes she is in love with him. An amulet, a medallion hanging around John's neck bearing the inscription "From Sylvia to Bruce," plays an important part in the story. Another girl—the girl next door—Clara Preston (Clara Bow) is secretly in love with John.

The two men rapidly develop into excellent fighter pilots and together they win a number of victories. Powell is shot down on one occasion but manages to crash his plane in no-man's-land and make his way safely back to his own lines.

On leave in Paris, John gets drunk. He meets Clara in a bar; she is working as a volunteer nurse in France. He is so drunk that he fails to recognize her, but she looks after him and sees that he gets back to his hotel. They spend the night together. When he awakens the next morning she is gone and he still does not know who she actually was.

After a time, Powell discovers that Sylvia is in love with Bruce. He considers himself a total failure and feels that his best friend has deceived him. In his frustration he begins to hate his former friend and avoids him as much as possible. They no longer fly together. But then one day they are ordered out on a mission together. They succeed in this task but are attacked by enemy fighter planes. During the dogfight, Powell deserts his friend and flies off. Alone, Armstrong is no match for the enemy planes and is shot down and subsequently reported missing.

Powell now realizes what a coward he has been and, as an outlet for his feelings, he takes off alone over enemy territory. He shoots at everything that crosses his path. Then, suddenly, he catches sight of an enemy plane. He attacks and a tough air battle ensues, until finally Powell sees the enemy plane crash. What he does not know is that he has shot down Bruce Armstrong. Armstrong had survived the previous dogfight, been forced down in enemy territory, and was piloting a stolen German plane back toward his own lines.

Armstrong's crashed Fokker (WINGS/1927).

John (Charles Rogers) discovers that he has shot down his best friend (WINGS/1927).

Powell sees the "German" crash on a small French farm. He spots a field nearby and lands his own plane. When he arrives at the wrecked aircraft he finds, to his distress, Bruce—fatally injured. He tries to help him, but it is too late and his friend dies in his arms.

The war soon ends and Powell, who has been flying in search of death up to the very end, returns to America. There he meets Sylvia and it is he who must tell her that her long wait for Bruce has been in vain. He also meets Clara and discovers that he has really been interested in her the whole time. They fall in love, and in the end it is she who helps him bear the burden of guilt for Armstrong's death. She never tells him of their brief meeting in the hotel in Paris.

Bruce (Richard Arlen) dies in the arms of his buddy (WINGS/1927).

The level of the film rises in the dramatic final scenes between the two friends, and Rogers and Arlen together give truly fine performances.

Wellman made a good film of *WINGS,* and a great flying film. Many of the aerial scenes are magnificent: the speed-packed "balloon" sequence, for instance; Powell's "one-man raid," and of course the highly exciting and wonderfully filmed final encounter between the two friends.

WINGS also represents the start of Wellman's career as a director of films on flying. In addition to other important achievements, he was to make many more flying stories during his remaining years in Hollywood.

A small role in *WINGS* was played with considerable bravura by a relatively unknown young man by the name of Gary Cooper. His performance as Cadet White, who is killed on his first solo flight, was excellent. Whether it was his acting or his personal charisma generally that gained him attention is not known, but obviously he made a good pilot since he played leading roles in two other flying films made in 1928—*THE LEGION OF THE CONDEMNED*, directed by Wellman, with Fay Wray as his leading lady, and *LILAC TIME* opposite Colleen Moore and Burr McIntosh, and directed by George Fitzmaurice.

It is still the war with the Germans that haunts these two films, and the flying sequences are well done and have plenty of action. The whole of *LILAC TIME* is played at a flying base in the vicinity of a French château. The daughter of this household, Jeannine (Colleen Moore), has placed the château at the disposal of the military. Seven flyers have been billeted in the place and one day one of them is reported missing. A replacement, Captain Philip Blythe (Cooper), arrives. Love soon blossoms between the young daughter of the château and the handsome pilot. But then one day he, too, crashes, right before the eyes of his beloved, who manages to pull him out of the wrecked plane and send him to the hospital. She is not allowed to go along with him in the ambulance, but she does come to the hospital later. She has a bouquet of lilacs with her, but a misunderstanding at the hospital makes Jeannine believe that Philip is already dead. She leaves the lilacs anyway and walks despondently away. But the flowers reach him and the film ends happily as he rushes out of the hospital, catches up to her and then takes her in his arms.

Fitzmaurice made *LILAC TIME* with a careful hand and it was quite a big success. The aerial photography was excellent and completely new to this film. The same camera technique was used in this film as in *WINGS*—the camera mounted ahead of the aft cockpit facing backward gave a definite feeling that it was the popular hero himself at the controls. The air battles were not as formidable as those in *WINGS*, but they were well done.

The air-battle sequences William Wellman used in *LEGION OF THE CONDEMNED* were virtually all "leftovers" from

Gary Cooper, Fay Wray and the German commandant (E. H. Calvert) in THE LEGION OF THE CONDEMNED (1928).

Gary Cooper is helped out of the wreckage by his own love—Colleen Moore. From LILAC TIME (1928).

WINGS. This did not mean that the effect was poor. On the contrary! The air battles and other flying sequences were of high quality.

In 1928 there was also *AIR PATROL,* produced by Universal, with Al Wilson. Actually, Wilson was a stunt pilot, one of the best in Hollywood. However, he played a number of leading roles, primarily in serial films which swamped the cinemas in the late twenties and early thirties. He was killed a few years later during a difficult exhibition of stunt flying.

The same year, *CAPTAIN SWAGGER* was also released, with Rod La Rocque and Sue Carol in the leading roles. It was directed by Edward H. Griffith and was a totally uninteresting bit of pap about a daring American pilot serving in the French air corps.

In 1929 George Hill made *THE FLYING FLEET* for Metro-Goldwyn-Mayer, with Ramon Novarro, Anita Page and Ralph Graves.

Fox also tried to milk this subject as long as possible and produced *SKY HAWK* in 1930, with John Garrick, Helen Chandler and Gilbert Emery in the leading roles. It was a weak film, the climax of which was an air battle over nighttime London between a German airship and the hero (Garrick) alone in his fighter plane (compare with *HELL'S ANGELS,* 1930). There was not much flying but a lot of romance. It is easy to understand Garrick's preoccupation—Miss Chandler was very beautiful.

In 1930 Paramount allowed Wellman to return to the Western Front. This time the film was called *YOUNG EAGLES* and was a one hundred percent sound film. Charles "Buddy" Rogers battled his way through this absolutely unbelievable story in which Jean Arthur was entangled as a female spy and Paul Lukas appeared as a charming German fighter pilot. The theme was otherwise much like *WINGS*—best friends kill each other in battle.

The egocentric multimillionaire Howard Hughes was a restless man. He was fascinated by flying and was a pilot himself. He wanted to make a *real* flying film, a film that would be remembered for all time. Sometime during 1927 he discussed the project with his friend, the director Marshall Neilan. They decided to begin with a film that would immortalize and glorify the feats of the Allied fighter pilots during the First World War.

THE SKY HAWK (1930).

Neilan, who had sketched out the main story for Hughes, wrote a synopsis but had nothing to do with the final screenplay. Hughes hired Harry Behn instead to write down Hughes's own ideas as they came to him and then the whole thing was left to Luther Reed to create a film drama.

Hughes chose James Hall and Ben Lyon for the leading roles, the Scandinavian actress Greta Nissen played the femme fatale. No expense was spared in acquiring authentic aircraft. Planes were brought from all over the world: Fokker D VIIs, Sopwith Camels, and S.E.5s. Complete flying bases were constructed in various parts of the United States to create the most authentic locations possible.

Hughes hired virtually all the well-known air acrobats and daredevils there were, and all the stunt pilots from Hollywood—except for the great specialist Dick Grace. He was

Charles Rogers and Paul Lukas in a dramatic sequence from YOUNG EAGLES (1930).

busy with the shooting of *LILAC TIME* and Howard Hawks's *THE AIR CIRCUS* (1928).

During the shooting of the air battles, which were filmed from a number of camera aircraft simultaneously, three pilots were killed. One crashed into a power line, another was killed when he ran out of fuel and crash-landed, and the third died in a Sikorsky S-29 (used as a Gotha bomber in the film) when it went into an uncontrollable spin.

HELL'S ANGELS was finally ready to be premiered in 1929. It had cost its producer approximately three million dollars although it was only a silent film. Yes, a silent film! Audiences were already spoiled by "talkies." "The most unforgettable flying film" was given a lukewarm reception both by the critics and audiences. The reviews were disastrous and Hughes decided immediately to withdraw it from circulation.

However, he did not let this fiasco ruin his investment but began immediately to remake the film—with sound.

During the shooting of the original version, Hughes himself had directed some scenes; now he took it over completely to do the "repair work." The dialogue was rewritten and all the dramatic scenes were reshot. Greta Nissen spoke English with a Scandinavian accent so she was removed and Hughes cast instead his latest "discovery," Jean Harlow, a blonde bombshell who secured her future in this film by establishing herself as a Hollywood star.

There were many supplementary flying scenes in addition to those shot for the original version. In the charity ball sequence, a two-color system in Technicolor was used that supplied an effective gimmick that was popular at the time in black-and-white films.

The premiere took place at Grauman's Chinese Theatre on Hollywood Boulevard. This was in June 1930 and the total cost of the film had now reached four million dollars, an astronomical sum for a single film at the time. Despite all the good intentions, the film was not really a success. The critics were still reserved—they found the flying scenes incredibly magnificent, but the story and presentation were execrable. The public, however, was rather more positive and it had a certain success in various parts of the world.

Ralph Graves standing beside Ramon Novarro (in cockpit). From THE FLYING FLEET (1929).

Although *HELL'S ANGELS* was considered to be a bad film, it must go down in the history of films about flying as an unforgettable adventure. The air battles are brilliantly filmed, almost exaggeratedly dramatic and realistic some of the time. The high point is the almost thirty minutes of a German airship in a night raid over London.

Briefly, the story is as follows: two American brothers by the name of Rutledge (James Hall and Ben Lyon) are studying at Oxford when World War I breaks out. They enroll in the Royal Flying Corps and are trained as fighter pilots. During their training, they attend a charity ball where they meet the beautiful Jean Harlow. The elder of the two brothers (Hall), who is both noble and idealistic, falls madly in love with her, but it is the younger of them (Lyon) who "draws the longest straw" and gets to see her home.

It is during the ensuing love scene that Miss Harlow delivers the well-known line:

From left: James Hall, Jean Harlow and Ben Lyon in HELL'S ANGELS (1930).

"Would you be shocked if I got into something more comfortable?" A line that, followed by the action, noticeably increased the pulse rate of every man in the audience. Whether Lyon was shocked or not history fails to mention because the camera backed discreetly off and faded out.

A German airship comes over London one night to bomb Trafalgar Square. It is a cloudy night and the Zeppelin remains above the clouds while a gondola is lowered 300 meters below it. There is a lookout in the gondola. It is fastened to the Zeppelin by a steel wire that is also the telephone connection with the Captain. The lookout's task is to lead the Zeppelin to its target, but this man has studied once at Oxford and his attachment to London is such that he deceives his Captain into dropping his bombs over Hyde Park instead—here they do no damage at all!

Four British fighter planes have now arrived on the scene and immediately attack the Zeppelin. The captain of the latter tries to gain speed and altitude by cutting the connecting wire to the gondola and ordering some members of the crew to abandon ship. He almost succeeds in escaping when the last remaining fighter plane—the other three have already been shot down—rams the airship and it crashes in flames. Quite magnificent!

James Hall (left) and Ben Lyon in HELL'S ANGELS (1930).

Our two heroes were among those who were shot down, but they both make forced landings to safety. They are now sent off to France to fly a captured German Gotha bomber. The aim is to use this aircraft in the bombing of an enemy ammunition dump. They take off on this mission but are attacked by none other than the Red Baron himself (who else?) and are shot down, but once again they survive—as prisoners of war, however.

The enemy believes that they know of plans for an impending Allied attack and they are threatened with execution if they do not reveal what they know. When Lyon's tongue has been loosened after being tortured, his own brother shoots him in order to stop important information being revealed to the enemy. Later, he himself is shot while trying to escape.

Despite its faults, *HELL'S ANGELS* was something of a public success, although it never reached the standard of *WINGS*. In a way, Howard Hughes achieved his goal—the film acquired lasting fame—although not for the reasons he had originally hoped. The critic "Sid" wrote in *Variety* on June 4, 1930: "It is not a sappy, imbecile tale. Neither may it be the greatest story which has ever been screened. Nevertheless, it has substance."

Howard Hawks, who had worked in Hollywood since 1918 both as a writer and film editor, had by 1929 directed ten or so films, among which was *THE AIR CIRCUS* (1928),

HELL'S ANGELS (1930).

THE DAWN PATROL (1930).

RICHARD
BARTHELMESS
The DAWN
PATROL
With
DOUGLAS
FAIRBANKS JR.
NEIL HAMILTON
FROM THE STORY "The Flight Commander"
by JOHN MONK SAUNDERS
ADAPTATION and DIALOGUE by HOWARD HAWKS
DAN TOTHEROH and SETON MILLER
DIRECTED BY
HOWARD HAWKS

and he wrote an original story together with John Monk Saunders for a film called *FLIGHT COMMANDER*. It was made for First National and renamed *THE DAWN PATROL*. The premiere was in 1930, with Richard Barthelmess, Douglas Fairbanks, Jr., and Neil Hamilton in the leading roles.

In *THE DAWN PATROL* we are back once again in France and the air battles between the Kaiser's air-arm and the Royal Flying Corps. Fighter ace Captain Courtney (Barthelmess) suddenly finds himself promoted to squadron leader when his predecessor, Major Brown (Hamilton), suffers a nervous breakdown. Courtney sees his pilots, all of them even younger than he is, disappear one after the other. They are all more or less still wet behind the ears, and when they arrive at the front with him they have little more than seven or eight hours flying time behind them. But they are enthusiastic and filled with confidence and believe they can perform miracles. Courtney knows better. He knows that they are green and that the enemy is efficient and ruthless. He knows that he is sending them to an almost certain death when he watches them take off on their first operation.

Douglas Fairbanks, Jr., and Richard Barthelmess in Howard Hawks's THE DAWN PATROL (1930).

Scott (Fairbanks, Jr.) as "the lost son" makes his unforgettable appearance at the mess. From THE DAWN PATROL (1930). *In the center: Barthelmess as Courtney.*

Like his predecessor, Courtney breaks down under the psychological burden he is forced to bear. However, together with his friend Lieutenant Scott (Fairbanks, Jr.), he manages somehow to hold out. Then Scott's younger brother joins the squadron and is shot down on his first mission. Because of this, the friendship between Courtney and Scott is broken, the squadron leader takes to the bottle and breaks down completely. Courtney goes out on a dangerous flight, which should have been done by Scott; he is shot down and dies in his burning plane. Scott now takes over the leadership of the squadron and the questionable privilege of aging before his time in this highly responsible position.

As a flying film, *THE DAWN PATROL* has much to recommend it! Action-packed air battles are interspersed with humorous scenes showing the special comradeship of flyers. It is also highly dramatic and shows, as does *WINGS, HELL'S ANGELS* and *YOUNG EAGLES,* the brutal pointlessness and madness of war.

BODY AND SOUL, based on a play called *Squadrons* by A. E. Thomas, was released in 1931 and directed by Alfred Santell. This film was made by Fox and it, too, depicted the air war in Europe between 1914 and 1918. Many American flyers came to Europe to fight under the Union Jack or Tricolor. In this story, Humphrey Bogart, Donald Dillaway and Charles Farrell join the Royal Flying Corps as fighter pilots. This was Bogart's third film in which he played a lead.

From left: Donald Dillaway, Charles Farrell and Humphrey Bogart in BODY AND SOUL (1931).

A short synopsis: Mal Andrews (Farrell), Jim Watson (Bogart) and Tap Johnson (Dillaway) arrive in England to enroll as pilots in the Royal Flying Corps. Watson has married just before leaving America. He becomes good friends with Mal and Tap. Jim is killed during an attack on a German reconnaissance balloon, but Mal, who has concealed himself on a plane without Jim's knowledge, destroys the balloon and sees to it that Jim gets the credit.

During a leave in England, Mal intends to give Jim's watch and some letters to a girl known as "Pom-Pom." Mal knows that Jim had an affair during his brief stay in England and assumes that it was with Pom-Pom.

A woman arrives at the hotel where Mal is staying; her name is Carla (Elissa Landi). Mal believes that she is Pom-Pom, and she

Spencer Tracy and William Boyd in SKY DEVILS (1932).

does not deny it. They soon become attached to each other and have an affair. During this time, Mal's squadron has suffered severe losses in battle and Tap is among those killed. To complicate things even more, Carla is accused of working for the enemy and Mal is suspected of being her accomplice. Another girl, Alice Lester (Myrna Loy), has also been accused by the Secret Service but denies that she is a spy. Carla is able to show, with the evidence of her letters to Jim, that she is his widow and that Alice is actually Pom-Pom and the real German spy—happy end!

BODY AND SOUL does not have a lot of flying, but it is a rather good film on its own terms.

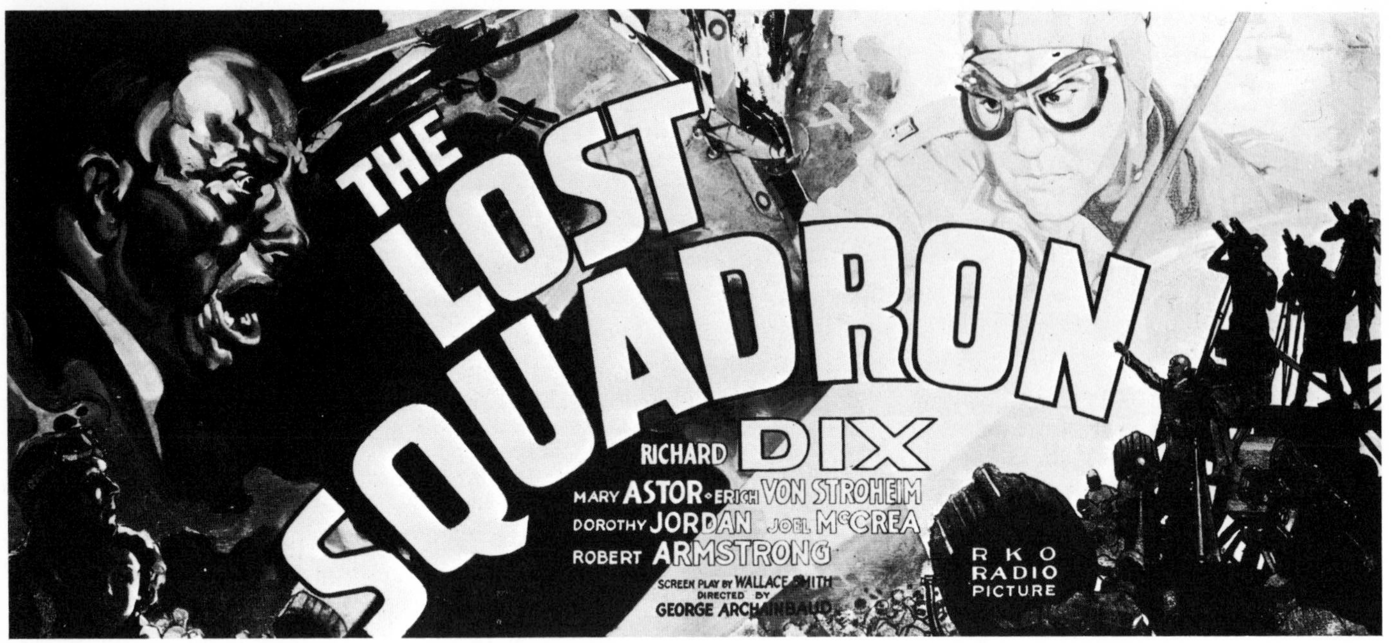

THE LOST SQUADRON (1932).

In 1931, George Hill directed *HELL DIVERS,* with Wallace Beery, Clark Gable, Dorothy Jordan and Conrad Nagel. And the following year—1932—Spencer Tracy, William Boyd and Ann Dvorak ended up in a more comic type of film produced by Howard Hughes. It was entitled *SKY DEVILS* and was a mixed bag of thousands of feet of filmed flying sequences left over from *HELL'S ANGELS.* Tracy's and Dvorak's rather charming and intelligent comedy scenes were mixed up in one great stew of air battles over the French trenches and bombing attacks on ammunition dumps. The film was directed by A. Edward Sutherland with the assistance of Howard Hawks.

Obviously Hughes believed that he had still not put all the leftover material to good use with this film and so released another grab bag the same year—*COCK OF THE AIR,* in which Chester Morris has an off-again, on-again affair with a seductive French girl (Billie Dove). The flying activity in this film was very restricted and the film generally was a rather spiritless affair.

Finally, a more peaceful movie: in 1932, Universal released *AIR MAIL,* with Pat O'Brien, Ralph Bellamy and Gloria Stuart. This film was directed by no less a personage than John Ford, but to no avail. It was a modern version of "Pony Express" and a rather poor one at that.

O'Brien is the tough guy who flies like the devil. He ignores virtually all the rules; the important thing is that the mail arrives on time. His boss (Bellamy) does not like his method of working and plans to fire him. However, Bellamy soon finds himself in serious trouble after a crash in the mountain wilderness. Rescue finally comes after many trials and tribulations and he is brought safely back to civilization by—who else?—the wild man he had despised so much.

A director by the name of George Archainbaud made in 1932 a sort of "semi-crime" story about flying called *THE LOST SQUADRON,* with Richard Dix, Mary Astor, Erich von Stroheim, Joel McCrea and Robert Armstrong in the cast.

This is rather a weak story about three stunt pilots who work in Hollywood for a temperamental and half-mad film director (von Stroheim). The latter discovers that one of the pilots (Dix) had once had a relationship with his present wife. Jealousy drives him to change the rudder cables on the aircraft Dix is to fly in a scene.

Fate intervenes and one of the other pilots (Armstrong) makes the flight instead of Dix. He crashes and is killed. The third pilot of

Facing page: Cary Grant and Fredric March in THE EAGLE AND THE HAWK *from 1933.*

Richard Barthelmess in CENTRAL AIRPORT (1933).

Fredric March in a very dramatic scene with Sir Guy Standing (THE EAGLE AND THE HAWK/1933).

the trio (McCrea) discovers von Stroheim's criminal trick and shoots him. In order to protect his buddy from the consequences of this killing, Dix loads the body into his plane, takes off, and then crashes with the body, killing himself in the process. The coast is then clear for McCrea to marry the woman he loves—not, however, the hated director's wife.

Basically it was a dreadful mixture with all the ingredients of a typical B-production, but with a number of good flying sequences—especially the crash-landings. It was, after all, about stunt pilots!

ACE OF ACES (1933) was about the brutalizing effects of war on the individual. A young sculptor suffers moral scruples about participating in the war. His girlfriend misinterprets this as a sign of cowardice and leaves him. To show her that she is wrong, he enters the conflict as a fighter pilot. After a period of time on the Western Front he has come to be regarded as one of the greatest flying aces, but in the meantime his personality has changed radically.

While on leave he meets his girlfriend again and tries to patch things up between them. But now she is shocked by how brutal and coarse he has become and leaves him once again.

Richard Dix gave perhaps one of his best performances in this film as the warm and gentle young man who is transformed into a cold-blooded killer. There was a fair amount of flying in this film but the direction of J. Walter Ruben was not adequate enough to lift it above the B-level.

William Wellman was again in action in 1933 with *CENTRAL AIRPORT*. He directed this film for First National, with Richard Barthelmess, Sally Eilers and Tom Brown in the leading roles.

It was hardly different from its predecessor but, on the other hand, *THE EAGLE AND THE HAWK* (same year) definitely was: This was another kind of flying film altogether. Directed by Stuart Walker and Mitchell Leisen, this film had action sequences that differed considerably from what one usually expected in this type of movie.

It was about human suffering and a neurotic military pilot who commits suicide. He takes his own life after he has made a rather passionate statement about the madness of war. It is a very dramatic, unglamorous film and its undertone of pacifism cannot be missed.

The tendency toward pacifism in American films could be found in a small group of vivid movies from the early thirties, such as Lewis Milestone's *ALL QUIET ON THE WESTERN FRONT* (1930), Frank Borzage's *NO GREATER GLORY* (1934), and Howard Hawks's *THE DAWN PATROL* (1930).

John Barrymore as the ruthless air company boss in Clarence Brown's airmail drama NIGHT FLIGHT (1934) *from the novel by Antoine de Saint-Exupéry.*

Fredric March gave a memorable performance in *THE EAGLE AND THE HAWK* as the young guilt-ridden flyer. His best friend was played by Cary Grant, and his loving, understanding girlfriend was portrayed by Carole Lombard.

The air-battle flying sequences are of less interest than the development of the characters; but they were well done, in most instances taken from *WINGS, DAWN PATROL,* and newsreels.

Airmail and passenger pioneers, particularly in South America, had been described in many books. This was a subject that offered much excitement and drama to the filmmaker.

French author Antoine de Saint-Exupéry wrote about these daring pilots with great intensity and poetry. His book *Vol de Nuit* was made into a fairly acceptable and interesting film in 1934 by Metro, under the title *NIGHT FLIGHT*. Clarence Brown directed it and the great John Barrymore appeared in it along with Clark Gable, Myrna Loy, Robert Montgomery and Lionel Barrymore.

A brief synopsis: Riviere (John Barrymore), head of a small airline called Air Express Company, believes that the nightly mail and passenger flights must continue, despite the opposition of his board of directors, even though the trips are very dangerous.

Riviere is incredibly harsh with his pilots. He has a will of steel and refuses to accept errors or lateness of flights. The slightest act of indiscipline and the person in question is either fined or fired. Deep inside, Riviere is really very committed to his pilots and only wants what is best for them. He becomes extremely depressed when he loses one of them, but he never shows this side of his personality.

During a dangerous flight in a storm with icing conditions, Fabian (Gable), one of the pilots, discovers that he only has enough fuel for another half-hour's flying. He transmits this over his radio, but tragedy is irrevocable. He is not heard again over the radio and Riviere is forced to tell Fabian's young wife (Loy) that her wait is in vain. But he has no time for a display of emotion and withdraws again into his shell. The company must survive and therefore the night flights must not only continue but increase in number. Future events prove him right.

Barrymore gives a virile portrayal of this lone wolf and has good support from the rest of the cast, although Gable's performance as Fabian was not one of his best. While the film cannot be considered great, it does have certain redeeming qualities. Even though Gable appeared in the film, it was not a great success among female audiences. It was aimed largely at those people who were interested in flying.

Apparently Myrna Loy enjoyed night flying, since in 1935 she appeared in James Flood's

Myrna Loy in WINGS IN THE DARK (1935).

Pat O'Brien and James Cagney were tough pilots in DEVIL DOGS OF THE AIR (1935).

WINGS IN THE DARK together with Cary Grant and Dean Jagger, but this time the action dealt mostly with stunt pilots. The same year Albert Rogell directed a bad film about mail flights for Columbia called *AIR HAWKS,* with Ralph Bellamy, Tala Birell and Douglas Dumbrille.

And also in the same year Warners released *CEILING ZERO,* a story about tough airline pilots, with James Cagney and Pat O'Brien as the civilian airmen. This company also had Cagney and O'Brien play together in *DEVIL DOGS OF THE AIR,* directed by Lloyd Bacon and concerned with the training of pilots for the American Marine Corps.

WEST POINT OF THE AIR dealt with the training of pilots for the U.S. Army Air Corps

James Cagney and June Travis appeared in Howard Hawks's CEILING ZERO (1935).

All landings are not happy landings. From WEST POINT OF THE AIR (1935).

Next page, left: Sally Eilers and Robert Armstrong in WITHOUT ORDERS (1936).

Next page, top right: FLIGHT FROM GLORY (1936)

In Wellman's MEN WITH WINGS (1938) *you could see Fred MacMurray in this warlike position. He is behind the machine guns of a Spad XIII.*

Next page, below: WINGS OVER HONOLULU (1937).

(USAAC), with Wallace Beery, Robert Young, Lewis Stone and Maureen O'Sullivan. It was shot at the flying school at Randolph Field in Texas, and Richard Rosson succeeded well in translating the screenplay of Frank Wead and Arthur J. Beckhard into a thrilling and enjoyable film. Incidentally, the original story was written by veteran John Monk Saunders.

A kind of "father-and-son drama" is played out. Big Mike (Beery), a flying instructor of the old school, wants his son, Little Mike (Young), to follow in his footsteps. The boy is not entirely uninterested but suffers from fear and a total lack of self-confidence. Nevertheless, he gives in to his father's wishes.

Following the passing of his officers' examination at West Point, he begins flying training. A variety of psychological problems arise, and after a considerable amount of flight drama and a goodly portion of romance the whole tale eventually reaches a happy end.

It was a straight, simple story, accurate in its description of the struggle of the young

Richard Dix in THE DEVIL'S SQUADRON (1936).

Pat O'Brien makes an overhaul on a Ford Trimotor in CHINA CLIPPER (1936).

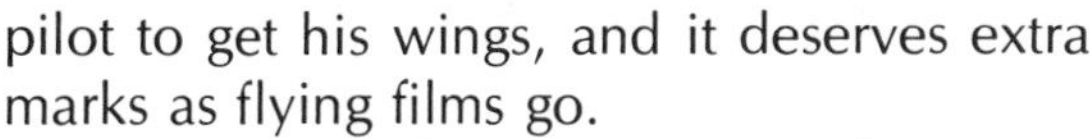

pilot to get his wings, and it deserves extra marks as flying films go.

Today, jets fly between New York and San Francisco in five and a half hours. The trip took considerably longer in 1936 when Paramount produced *13 HOURS BY AIR*. The hero and heroine in this film about a record transcontinental flight were played by Fred MacMurray and Joan Bennett. It was directed by Mitchell Leisen, a very talented Hollywood veteran.

Also released in 1936, Erle C. Kenton's *DEVIL'S SQUADRON*, with Richard Dix and Lloyd Nolan, offered some thrilling flying sequences.

The same was true of RKO's *FLIGHT FROM GLORY*, directed by Lew Landers, with Chester Morris, Whitney Bourne, Van Heflin, and Onslow Stevens, and also *WITHOUT ORDERS*, with Robert Armstrong and Sally Eilers, and directed by Louis Friedlander (i.e., Lew Landers).

Then Warners-First National drew an ace. This was *CHINA CLIPPER*, an excellent story about the big flying boats that traveled the long Pacific route during the thirties. Pat O'Brien, Ross Alexander, Humphrey Bogart and others were fairly convincing in their roles. The distaff side was taken care of by Beverly Roberts and Marie Wilson.

The aerial photography was remarkably

beautiful, particularly on the long test flight from Alameda, California, via Honolulu, Midway, Wake Island, Guam and Manila to Macao. The cinematographers of Warners and the pilots of Pan American Airways did an excellent job, and it was great advertising.

The Adventures of Jimmie Allen, a popular radio series, was the basis for another film of 1936, *THE SKY PARADE.* The plot deals with former fighter pilots who turn to circus flying and other adventures in the postwar years. Eventually, they end up as pioneers among American passenger plane pilots. The film was well-received by critics.

Jimmie Allen, then 18, played the lead role. Also in the cast were William Gargan, Kent Taylor and Katherine DeMille. Otho Lovering directed for Paramount.

At Universal, a director called H.C. Potter made an acceptable film about aircraft carriers. The year was 1937 and *WINGS OVER HONOLULU* provided a good description of how the latest leviathans of the U.S. Navy functioned. Ray Milland, Kent Taylor and William Gargan soared up into the blue above the *Saratoga* and *Lexington,* while the beautiful Wendy Barrie waited anxiously on terra firma.

Milland used his flight knowledge again in 1938 in *MEN WITH WINGS,* in which he played against Fred MacMurray. The woman they fought over was Brenda Marshall. Color film had finally arrived in flying films, too, and William Wellman made, as usual, a thrilling and enjoyable movie.

Amazons of the air were introduced in

Constance Bennett looks very beautiful as a female pilot in TAIL SPIN (1938).

MEN WITH WINGS (1938). *From left: Ray Milland, Louise Campbell and Fred MacMurray.*

AEROMOTIV
SERV
STORAGE
RACES
PILOT

1938 in *TAIL SPIN,* in which Alice Faye, Constance Bennett and Nancy Kelly played tough racer pilots who went through a variety of adventures under the direction of Roy Del Ruth.

In RKO's *SKY GIANT* from the same year, Lew Landers called the shots while Chester Morris and Richard Dix competed for the charms of Joan Fontaine.

In 1938 there was also a film drama about test pilots, appropriately titled *TEST PILOT,* produced by and excellently directed by Victor Fleming.

In this film Myrna Loy is wooed by two test-pilot friends, Clark Gable and Spencer Tracy. It was an exciting tale and the flying sequences are really thrilling. The denouement is reached during an advanced test on the completely new Boeing B-17 Flying Fortress, which was being tested for the American Bomber Command.

With a heavy ballast of sandbags, Gable, with Tracy as his copilot, climbs to a great height, but the aircraft cannot stand up to the strain and peels off into a steep dive. The lashings come loose and the cargo of sand shifts in the plane. The center of gravity changes drastically and they dive out of control. They try to parachute out, but once Gable is safely out Tracy becomes pinned down by the sandbags and is killed as he goes down with the plane.

Despite the advent of such modern aircraft as the Flying Fortress, film producers were still haunted by the First World War. *DAWN PATROL,* the old film by John Monk Saunders and Howard Hawks, first made in 1930, was remade in 1938 by Warners, under the direction of Edmund Goulding. Goulding's version was one of the most unforgettable flying films ever made. The content of Hawks's success remained unchanged, but the dialogue was partially rewritten by Seton I. Miller and Goulding.

Alice Faye also flew in TAIL SPIN (1938).

Clark Gable, Myrna Loy and Spencer Tracy in the Metro number of 1938—TEST PILOT.

Errol Flynn (as Courtney) in the cockpit of his Nieuport 24. From THE DAWN PATROL (1938).

David Niven and Errol Flynn in Edmund Goulding's version of THE DAWN PATROL (1938).

Warners gave the lead to its biggest star, Errol Flynn, who played the young squadron leader Courtney. Flynn gave one of his best performances. His popularity was enormous at the time, following his successes in *Captain Blood* (1935), *The Charge of the Light Brigade* (1936) and *The Adventures of Robin Hood* (1938).

Two of his fellow players were Basil Rathbone and David Niven. As always, Rathbone gave a remarkable performance, this time as the neurotic Major Brand, who was Courtney's predecessor as squadron leader. Courtney's best friend, Scott, was played by David Niven, the charming, attractive Englishman who had made his name in the story of the perfect British butler Jeeves, *Thank You, Jeeves* (1936).

Scott's entrance into the mess after having been reported missing is unforgettable. Clad in polka-dot pajamas, a leather jacket and an extravagantly long "Richthofen scarf," he storms in, tired and dirty but with a wide grin across his whole face. In his arms he carries a number of bottles of champagne, and his return to his comrades, just when they were drinking a toast in his memory, becomes very hearty but just a little too jovial, perhaps.

The flying sequences were excellent and those who had seen the first version perhaps recognized them. In fact, many of the flying scenes from the first film were used in the second, together with completion material

Flynn, right, talks with Morton Lowry (as Scott's younger brother) in THE DAWN PATROL (1938).

In TODAY WE LIVE (1933) *we saw (from left) Roscoe Karns, Gary Cooper and Robert Young.*

Randolph Scott (left) and Robert Shaw in Alfred E. Green's 20,000 MEN A YEAR (1939).

that was well matched into the action. The lone raid of Courtney and Scott on the German airbase, for instance, was made with the aid of models. Other new material was Court's crash landing in a Camel aircraft. However, these latter sequences were not mock-ups but were shots of real stunt pilots.

Flynn and Niven worked beautifully together, both in the scenes of light humor and in the more dramatic and tragic scenes in the latter part of the film. In these, they share the experiences of utter hopelessness and absurdity in what they are doing—fighting and sending their friends to their death. The pacifist undertones in *DAWN PATROL* came at the time of the approach to World War II.

There was a film made in 1938, premiering in 1939, about the training of a new generation of airline pilots. It was called *20,000 MEN A YEAR* and was directed by Alfred E. Green. The male leads were played by Randolph Scott, Preston Foster, and Robert Shaw, and to ensure these gentlemen a reasonable taste of love, Margaret Lindsay and Mary Healy were included in the cast. It was not a great film, but there were a number of thrills and the air photography was exceptional for the period.

Universal also presented two films in the genre at the time. The first, *LEGION OF THE LOST FLYERS,* was directed by Christy Cabanne and starred Richard Arlen, Anne Nagel and Andy Devine. The second, *PIRATES OF THE SKIES,* directed by Joe MacDonaugh, with Kent Taylor and Rochelle Hudson in the leading roles, was a particularly unpraiseworthy effort.

Columbia also checked in with a flying film in 1939. *TRAPPED IN THE SKY* concerned sabotage within the air corps. Lewis D. Collins directed. In the cast were Katherine DeMille, Jack Holt and C. Henry Gordon.

We have now reached the beginning of a new decade, but before we go on we should mention briefly a few additional films that were made in the thirties. There were, in fact, quite a few films in which flying played a considerable part in the background action. These sequences consisted almost exclusively of borrowed or leftover segments of older films with a World War I milieu.

For example, a large amount of footage from Howard Hughes's *HELL'S ANGELS* was used in such productions as Victor Flemings's *THE WHITE SISTER* (1933), with Clark Gable and Helen Hayes, and Metro's *TODAY WE LIVE* (1933), directed by Howard Hawks and starring Gary Cooper and Joan Crawford.

Fox, too, borrowed most of the flying sequences in *HELL IN THE HEAVENS* from *HELL'S ANGELS*. It was released in 1934 and was directed by John Blystone; in it, Warner Baxter played a veteran pilot who suffered nightmares about being shot down by an enemy flying ace—"the Baron."

Ben Lyon and James Bush took to the air in *CRIMSON ROMANCE* (1934).

William Dieterle borrowed some of the flying sequences for *THE LAST FLIGHT* (1931) from Hawks's *DAWN PATROL*. It was made by First National and had Richard Barthelmess, Johnny Mack Brown, David Manners and Elliott Nugent playing a gang of pilot drifters, and Helen Chandler as the lady who ends up with Barthelmess after all his buddies have been killed.

Metro's *SUZY* (1936) was directed by George Fitzmaurice and starred Franchot Tone, Jean Harlow and Cary Grant. It was more of a spy-love drama than a flying story. However, the flying sequences included in it were borrowed from Hughes's "unforgettable" spectacle of 1930.

During the ten-year period following *WINGS*, the cinema audience had learned a great deal about the world of flying and about flying itself—particularly the more warlike kind.

The movie industry could, however, face the future with some confidence—there would be a considerable number of films about flying—since producers and directors had succeeded in putting wings on their stars.

Romance again—this time Jean Harlow and Cary Grant in SUZY (1936).

Time of Darkness

In Europe, the political climate was rapidly changing. The Führer, Adolf Hitler, had already marched into Austria and brought the Sudetenland Germans of Czechoslovakia under his rule. Europe was in a state of terrible suspense.

Despite the tense political situation—or perhaps because of it—more films were made during this period than ever before. There was also a notable interest in the political events of the day. The films of the time were often made against a military background, and a certain element of patriotism and propaganda crept into them. This was true not just of German films but also of other European productions. American films had not yet felt—with a few exceptions—the hot wind of change from the Old World. The Spanish Civil War was just ending, but the feeling was general that a new war was close at hand.

Mit Eichenlaub und Schwerten

During the thirties and forties there were a number of flying films produced in Germany, which are of some interest despite their obvious political propaganda.

RIVALEN DER LUFT (Rivals of the Air) was made by UFA and directed by Frank Wisbar, with Claus Clausen, Wolfgang Liebeneiner, Hilde Gebühr and Sybille Schmitz. It concerns two young people, Karl and his girlfriend Christine (Clausen and Gebühr), who are crazy about "soaring" and do everything they can to learn to fly. Karl even designs his own plane which is approved and subsequently built. He intends to use this plane in a flying competition, but before this a number of technical problems and romantic entanglements develop. A pretty female pilot (Schmitz) arouses Christine's jealousy by displaying an interest in Karl, to which he responds. Christine in turn is loved secretly by her flying instructor whose name is Willi (Liebeneiner). Everything turns out well in the end; they all find their respective loves and Karl wins the five-thousand-marks prize in the gliding competition.

This beautiful air shot of a Messerschmitt Bf 109 comes from the West German film DER STERN VON AFRIKA (1957) (The Star of Africa).

Then came *ZIEL IN DEN WOLKEN (Lost in the Clouds)* (1938), by Terra Film. This time around Wolfgang Liebeneiner stood behind the camera rather than in front of it—as director of the film about German, French, and British aviation pioneers. Included in the cast were Albert Matterstock, Leny Marenback and Brigitte Horney.

The story concerned a young officer of the guards, Walter von Suhr (Albert Matterstock), who has his career all staked out. However, an interest in flying is awakened within him when he witnesses the landing of a plane at Johannisthal. Here he meets the owner of the aircraft along with the not-yet-famous pilots, Latham, Farman and Bleriot.

He realizes that flying could have great military potential in the future and tries to get his regimental commander interested in it. The latter is very cool towards the idea and Walter decides to resign his officer's commission and devote all his time to aviation. The year is 1909, and his girlfriend Tilde, who admires him because he shows the courage of his convictions, becomes engaged to him. His father, on the other hand,

A little bit moist below!? . . . From the German RIVALEN DER LUFT (1934) (Rivals of the Air).

Albert Matterstock and Leny Marenbach in ZIEL IN DEN WOLKEN (1938) (Toward the Clouds).

disapproves of Walter's behavior and threatens to disinherit him if he does not come to his senses.

Despite these threats, Walter continues to fight for what he believes in. Although he is short of cash, he manages somehow to acquire a plane of his own, but unfortunately it has a great many mechanical bugs. But soon these are ironed out and our hero achieves his goal: to soar up into the air in his own plane. At last von Suhr senior grasps that his son has "a vocation" and, as the crowning touch, Walter receives word that the army is now greatly interested in flying and that his old regiment is planning to set up a flying squadron—if he wishes, he is welcome to return and take over this new "advanced weapon" and continue his career as an officer.

Paul Hartmann in POUR LE MÉRITE (1938).

At a regimental parade, he is asked to land his machine in the presence of the general and his staff as a symbol of the arrival of a new era. At his side in the aircraft is—naturally!—Tilde, who has so bravely helped him through this difficult time.

In 1938, a film was made that differed considerably from the run of the mill. This was Karl Ritter's *POUR LE MÉRITE* which, notwithstanding its palpably Nazi undertones, can be regarded as a technically good film about flying. Ritter himself was a fighter pilot during World War I and he had made a fine documentary about fighter pilots in the hell of the Western Front. It told about the survivors who came to form the backbone of the new Germany and its new flying corps—the Luftwaffe.

The film was permeated with patriotic fervor and, in spite of its glorification of the Nazi cause, it compelled the spectator's attention. Paul Hartmann was magnificent as the squadron leader and he received much assistance from the other "flyers," Albert Hehn, Fritz Kampers and Herbert A. E. Böhme.

A brief résumé of the story: a German fighter squadron which had fought bravely and effectively during the final phase of the war suddenly finds itself in an entirely new world—a world at peace. The commander

Hermann Braun as Eckhard in Herbert Maisch's D III 88 *(1938). The aircraft is an old "Iron Jenny"—Junkers Ju 52.*

1/581
Tobis Film-V

Kampfgeschwader Lützow

TOBIS

POUR LE MÉRITE (1938). *A.E. Böhme was a real pilot of WWI. Here you can see him appearing as a film lieutenant wearing the new Luftwaffe uniform. The aircraft behind are Heinkel He 51s.*

of the squadron (Hartmann) refuses to surrender to the enemy. He takes his pilots and aircraft back to Germany—a fairly useless gesture, since once there he witnesses them being destroyed by the "Red Revolution" which is rapidly tightening its grip on the German people. The pilots spread out over the whole of the Fatherland and separately struggle through the Depression years of starvation, inflation and other miseries. Then comes a new wave of revolution—and National Socialism.

The film ends with the old commandant from the Western Front being assigned to lead a new fighter wing by no less a personage than Göring himself. In the final scenes he is seen reviewing his new wing equipped with the most modern fighter plane available—the Messerschmitt Me 109.

Also in 1938 came Herbert Maish's *D III 88*, with Christian Kayssler, Otto Wernicke, Heinz Welzel and Hermann Braun. It showed the daily life of a German fighter pilot as it was just prior to the outbreak of World War II, and dealt with presence of mind, comradeship and—more than anything else—discipline.

KAMPFGESCHWADER LÜTZOW (1940) (Bomber Wing Lützow).

Two young flyers, Fritz Paulsen (Welzel) and Robert Eckhard (Braun), are the very best of friends and are both considered to be very promising pilots. A misunderstanding occurs and they become bitter enemies (obviously not an uncommon theme).

During a night flight over Germany they fly, against orders, into an area of bad weather with fog and icing conditions. Their battle against the weather is very dramatic and convincingly presented, as is the highly charged atmosphere in the cockpit of the plane. The flight ends in a crash, not especially serious, but the two men, who through their private enmity have disregarded military discipline, risk their chances for promotion. They are both grounded and no longer allowed to take part in military exercises. But the comradeship which exists among the flyers now comes to their aid. An old non-commissioned officer (Wernicke)

Top: Hermann Braun (as Eckhard) and Heinz Welzel (as Paulsen) leave their crashed and sinking machine. From the German D III 88 *(1938).*

Center: KAMPFGESCHWADER LÜTZOW (1940) (Bomber Wing Lützow).

Below, from left: Hermann Braun, Adolf Fischer, Horst Birr and Heinz Welzel in KAMPFGESCHWADER LÜTZOW (1940).

who was at the front in the war succeeds in talking the wing commander (Kayssler) into having second thoughts. The two young hotheads are entrusted by him to carry out an important mission, a task in which they are eminently successful.

D III 88 must be classed among good films about flying. It has a simple, exciting story and the flying sequences are of high filmic quality. Nor is the film heavily burdened with pure Nazi propaganda, although this certainly seeps through occasionally; after all, the film is concerned with discipline—ruthless, mechanical discipline and self-sacrifice.

This film was followed by a sequel which was released in 1940 under the title *KAMPFGESCHWADER LÜTZOW (Bomber Wing Lützow).* Tobis Film, which had produced *D III 88,* now had Hans Bertram direct the sequel. The main cast was the same as in the earlier film: Kayssler, Welzel, Braun. Also appearing were Hannes Keppler and Marietheras Angerpointer in two important subordinate roles.

The story is still about the same two inseparable friends, Eckard and Paulsen, who are now attached to a bomber squadron under their old leader, Colonel Mithoff (Kayssler). The action all takes place during a few days in August 1939. It is a time when the Luftwaffe is under battle orders. The wing is ordered to fly toward Poland.

A quotation from *Illustrierter Filmkurir* reads: "The die is cast! The flyers of Lützow rise in their grey birds and set their course toward the East. In spectacular scenes the vast wonder of the eighteen-day battle unfolds over the silver screen. The German Ministry of Defence itself is responsible for the military participation in this film and the battle scenes we see are authentic ones. The tanks and aircraft are not just mock-ups, they are the real thing—in a real war."

Obviously the film is clear propaganda, but nevertheless it is rather fair in its description of the young men who are forced eventually to attack England.

"The flyers of Lützow are never long at rest—despite the formidable resistance of

Heinz Rühmann in QUAX IN AFRIKA (1945), *originally called* QUAX IN FAHRT.

the British air force, the heroic spirit of the German pilots cannot be broken."

Eckhard and Paulsen, both in love with the same girl, are put through severe tests of courage in the final reel, and the film ends in the way films of this type usually do. Paulsen is known for his efficiency as a pilot, but during an attack he is wounded. Dying now, he displays his sense of responsibility for his aircraft and his loyalty to his comrades up to the very end. He returns the plane and its crew safely to base.

At this time the German film industry was already deeply infiltrated by the views of the Minister of Propaganda (Goebbels). However, many of the films then made have other qualities to recommend them and that make them interesting and worthy of the attention of the moviegoer.

For example, Kurt Hoffman made an amusing film comedy about flying in 1941—*QUAX, DER BRUCHPILOT*—with Heinz Rühmann, Karin Himboldt and Harry Liedtke.

Otto Groschembügel, nicknamed "Quax," is a clerk in a travel agency. He wins first prize in a competition: free flying training at the school at Bergried. The pilot pupils are expected to show great enthusiasm for flying, and Quax, who has landed in the school by sheer accident, makes himself unbearable from the very first day. He is expelled, and the reason given is that he lacks feeling for flying and has no sense of discipline.

When Quax returns home, he discovers that his girlfriend has gone off with somebody else—the rich Herr Busse. He realizes that, whether he likes it or not, he must become a pilot. But they will not take him back at Bergried. Quax may have shown himself wanting as a student flyer but he is not lacking in ingenuity. While at a party he invites his new girl and a couple of village children to a flight in a balloon that belongs to the flying school. Although this was a thoughtless prank, he handles the balloon well and everything turns out all right. The head of the flying school, who has witnessed Quax's flight in the balloon, is impressed by his ability to maneuver it and so tempers justice with mercy and allows Quax to reenter the flying school. Quax proves that he is now more mature and turns out to be a good pilot. He wins the admiration of his instructors and fellow students and in the next flying course Quax has become one of the instructors.

This film was perhaps more of a farce than one would expect of a flying film, but it was amusing—to a large extent thanks to the very funny Heinz Rühmann.

In *STUKAS* (1941), Karl Ritter depicted the life of pilots in battle with great authenticity. But the film was really rather horrifying. It showed one of the most beastly and hated weapons used in the opening phase of the Second World War—Junkers Ju 87 Stuka. This was a dive-bomber that spread terror and destruction over a large part of Europe. The German pilots gained great victories with it in the beginning, but their luck soon changed and this aircraft became a "sitting duck" for Allied fighter pilots.

Carl Raddatz played the lead as Hauptmann Bork, who led his victorious young flying hussars in crushing attacks on the enemy. A rather macabre sequence in the film

Lothar Firman helps his student and fellow "Quax" out of the airplane after a wild ride in the air. From QUAX DER BRUCHPILOT (1941).

Karl Raddatz as Hauptman Bork in Karl Ritter's STUKAS *from 1941.*

The medical orderly takes care of a slightly injured Karl Raddatz in the German film STUKAS (1941).

Hubert Kiurina (left) a. Hannes Stelzer in Ritter's BESATZUNG DORA (1943) (The Dora Crew).

Gunnar Möller (center) in JUNGE ADLER (1944) (Young Eagles).

occurs when the Stuka squadron is on its way to new targets and all the pilots begin to sing the "Stuka song" over their radios. It is sung, in the manner of the time, at a frisky march tempo. The song was written by Herbert Windt, the favorite composer of Nazi propagandists. He also wrote the music to *MORGENROT* (1933), *TRIUMPH DES WILLENS* (1935), and *OLYMPIA* (1938) plus many of Ritter's films: *UNTERNEHMEN MICHAEL* (1937), *POUR LE MÉRITE* (1938), and *KADETTEN* (1941), to name only a few.

Whether he was a good composer or not, Herbert Windt's attempt to lift *STUKAS* to the level of operetta was rather maladroit, although certainly most of the responsibility must lie with Ritter. Elsewhere, music played an important part in German films of the time, not merely as a means of emphasizing the propaganda but also to raise the artistic value and provide another dimension to the pictorial drama.

In 1942, Roger von Norman, probably in an uninspired moment, directed a film about the Hitler Youth—*HIMMELHUNDE (Sky Dogs).* It was not very original and dealt with the same subject as always—obedience, unquestioned obedience!

A young man who belongs to a sailplane club, included in a Hitler Youth Group, wins

Facing page: Helmut Kautner's DES TEUFELS GENERAL (1955) (The Devil's General).

The crew left their Ju 88 after a mission. From BESATZUNG DORA (1943).

Des
Teufels General

Curd Jürgens as General Harras in DES TEUFELS GENERAL (1955) (The Devil's General).

a flying competition with a borrowed sailplane. He had, however, been forbidden to use the plane. Despite the fact that he wins the competition, he is punished. He has disobeyed orders, broken a trust. It is more important to obey orders than to win prizes, fame and honor.

Despite the thinness of the plot, a full-length film was made, since it takes some time to get our young "hero" to shape up. He must be brought to his senses—he is to become a Luftwaffe pilot and disobedience will not be tolerated. And then one fine soaring day he has finally learned to "sit upright"—he has become a well-drilled little Nazi, right to the tips of his fingers.

Karl Ritter had shown earlier that he was a relatively good director of flying films and in 1943 he made *BESATZUNG DORA (The Dora Crew)* for UFA. This film was banned by the censors and never shown. The reason for this was that Germany's situation worsened implacably at the turn of the year 1943–44. This was especially true on the Eastern Front where the action of the film took place.

The leading figure in the film, Lieutenant Joachim Krane (Hannes Stelzer), dreams of settling down with his girlfriend after the war on a farm in occupied Russia—a dream that was unconvincing to the German people at a time when neither the German high command nor even Hitler himself were able to believe in victory over the Red Army.

Facing page: DER STERN VON AFRIKA (1957) (The Star of Africa).

However, those who have seen the film consider that it had some impressive technical qualities and that the flying sequences were first class. The actors appearing in *BESATZUNG DORA* were Hannes Stelzer, Hubert Kiurina, Josef Dahmen, Suse Graf and Ernst von Klipstein, among others.

A good journeyman job was done in 1944 by Alfred Weidenmann in another film about the Hitler Youth entitled *JUNGE ADLER (Young Eagles).* It concerned the obstinate son of an airplane manufacturer who learns proper discipline by joining the Hitler Youth flying division and being sent to work in his father's factory. It was, of course, another big propaganda number—and what film at that time was not?—but it was beautifully photographed and provided an unusually powerful and straightforward description of "young boys being fashioned into men." A fashioning, alas, which was based on a gravely fallacious ideal, even though in this particular film the deadening, mechanical discipline was not spread on too thickly.

During 1945 a sequel was made to the film about the little flying comedian Quax. Its title was *QUAX IN FAHRT* (also called

JOACHIM HANSEN
MARIANNE KOCH
HERZOG FILMVERLEIH
DER
STERN
VON
AFRIKA
Ein ALFRED WEIDENMANN-Film mit HANSJÖRG FELMY · KARL LANGE · PEER SCHMIDT
HORST FRANK · ALEXANDER KERST · ALBERT HEHN · GISELA VON COLLANDE · ARNO PAULSEN
REGIE: ALFRED WEIDENMANN · Drehbuch: Herbert Reinecker nach einem Stoff von Udo Wolter · Bild: Helmuth Ashley · Musik: Hans-Martin Majewski

A flight (schwarme) of Messerschmitt 109s return to their base in the desert. From DER STERN VON AFRIKA (1957) (The Star of Africa).

QUAX IN AFRIKA), but it was not shown until 1953.

In this film, Heinz Rühmann was involved more in romantic affairs than flying, but he was still a flying instructor at the flying school at Bergried. He was also involved in a number of adventures in darkest Africa together with Herta Feiler, Karin Himboldt and Bruni Löbel. It was produced by Terra Film and directed by Helmuth Weiss.

After the war was over, it was not until 1957—for obvious reasons—that a new German film about flying appeared on the screen. Curd Jürgens had, of course, played the flying German General Harras in *DES TEUFELS GENERAL (The Devil's General)* (1955) but it was a rather pale version of a flying film. It was based on Carl Zuckmayer's drama and was austerely directed by Helmut Käutner, although some scenes were vividly acted—and from a purely technical point of view one had the opportunity of seeing a squadron of unusual Junkers' Ju 86 bombers. These planes, which were used in only a few wings of the Luftwaffe during the war in Germany, were chartered from Sweden, the only country in the world at that time with this particular aircraft still in service.

Jürgens' portrayal of Harras was well done and Zuckmayer's story, about a general and pilot who hates the Party and sees through the charlatan Hitler, had definite parallels with the life of one of the great figures in German aviation history—General Ernst Udet.

In any case, a real flying adventure appeared in 1957 when it was abruptly decided that the heroes of the Luftwaffe should be honored. The film was called *DER STERN VON AFRIKA (The Star of Africa)* and was about one of the greatest German fighter aces of the Second World War, Hans Joachim Marseille.

The purpose of the film was to glorify Marseille's name. It was badly directed by Alfred Weidenmann. Marseille died in the desert when returning from an air battle. The plane—a Messerschmitt 109—developed engine trouble and caught fire. Marseille tried to bring the aircraft back behind his own lines but stayed with it too long. When he finally tried to parachute out, his plane was evidently too close to the ground, or perhaps he hit the tail section and was knocked unconscious? No one knows for sure, but his comrades never saw his chute open. Marseille's body was found six kilometers behind his own lines. He was buried there.

He was twenty-three at the time of his death, a captain and Germany's leading fighter ace, with 152 enemy planes to his credit. He had been awarded the most distinguished medals it was possible to receive, among which were Der Ritterkreutz mit Eichenlaub Schwerten und Diamanten.

The leading role was played by Joachim

Joachim Hansen as Hauptmann Marseille in DER STERN VON AFRIKA (1957). *The crashed machine is a Messerschmitt Bf 109.*

Hansen, whom critics maintained gave a convincing impression of the idolized young pilot. Included in the cast were Hansjöerg Felmy, Horst Frank and Marianne Koch.

We would like to mention as a curiosity that the Spanish Air Force was able to supply all the types of aircraft that were needed in the film, including real Messerschmitt 109s, Heinkel 111s and a couple of Ju 52s.

Although the film offered a considerable amount of flying, from a purely technical point of view it was mediocre. Also, it was largely a vehicle for the glorification of its hero—and for political reasons it was banned in Germany. Marseille was clearly a Nazi pilot. Included in the cast were Hansjörg still not considered suitable—at least in some circles—for the spotlight (something to do with a bad conscience?). But *DER STERN VON AFRIKA* has been shown in a number of countries outside Germany and both information and stills are available.

Peter van Eyck as "flugkapitän" in ABSCHIED VON DEN WOLKEN (1959) (Farewell to the Clouds).

A film titled *ABSCHIED VON DEN WOLKEN (Farewell to the Clouds)* was released in 1959; it was directed by Gottfried Reinhardt. This movie cannot really be fitted into the category of flying films, but is closely related to the subject since much of the action occurs on board a passenger plane over Bermuda.

The passengers are of various nationalities and dispositions: a revolutionary general fleeing his country with most of its cash, an old Nazi, and a Dutch adventurer, to name only a few. There is also a beautiful stewardess (Sonja Ziemann).

Together the general and the Nazi cause the captain of the plane (Peter van Eyck) and his crew some trouble. However, the Dutch adventurer (O.W. Fischer) straightens everything out in the end and provides some exciting final minutes with a belly landing of the plane as the climax.

U.S.NAVY
3-B-15
U.S.NAVY
3-B-14
SB2U-1
0739
U.S.NAVY
3
13
13

The Eagle and the Lion

The Old World was once again set on fire and the German war machine began to pound little England. One could see that Great Britain was not totally unprepared by the film *THE LION HAS WINGS,* which was produced by Alexander Korda's London Films in 1939 and directed by a trio consisting of Michael Powell, Brian Desmond Hurst and Adrian Brunel. It was a dramatic semi-documentary film starring Ralph Richardson, Merle Oberon and June Duprez.

Another British film from the same period was *Q-PLANES* with Ralph Richardson, Laurence Olivier and Valerie Hobson in the leading roles. It was directed by Tim Whelan and was about a newly constructed bomber that mysteriously disappears on its test flight—actually, a number of planes disappear. Scotland Yard is called in and Major Hammond (Richardson) takes over the case and soon solves the mystery. It transpires that a mad scientist has lured the planes off course with a radio transmitter and forced them to land. He then holds the crews prisoner.

Richardson receives help from Olivier in catching the thief, but the latter gave a rather pale performance as the test pilot McVane. Valerie Hobson was seen as Hammond's beautiful sister, and a love affair between her and the daring test pilot could not, of course, be avoided.

Facing page: A flight of Vought-Sikorsky SB2U-1 Vindicators fly "line abreast" in WINGS OF THE NAVY (1939).

Below, left: A Vickers Wellington takes off for a mission in THE LION HAS WINGS (1939).

Below, right: The British Q-PLANES (1939) *with Laurence Olivier (in cockpit), George Curzon (left), and David Tree.*

The United States, not having entered the war yet, was still preoccupied with peaceful subjects. A return to the heroic mail pilots was accomplished by Howard Hawks in 1939 with *ONLY ANGELS HAVE WINGS.* This was a well made and original film drama about flying in South America in the thirties, set against the terrifying background of the high Andes. Hawks was helped greatly by Cary Grant, Jean Arthur, Thomas Mitchell and most of all perhaps by Richard Barthelmess as the lost pilot. A young girl by the name of Rita Hayworth was seen in a small role, a girl of whom much would be heard later.

ONLY ANGELS belongs on this author's list of classics: it has warmth, humor; the external excitement is counterpointed by an inner tension; the excellent action sequences are never allowed to interfere with the penetrating insight into the characters.

In *WINGS OF THE NAVY,* made the same year, Warners and Lloyd Bacon showed that the United States was also prepared for war, and appearing as the salty flyers were George Brent, John Payne, Victor Jory and Frank McHugh. The role of the ever-patient, lady-in-waiting was played by Olivia de Havilland.

In 1940 Lewis Seiler made *FLIGHT ANGELS* for Warners, a fairly exciting but rather

FLIGHT ANGELS (1940).

thin story about the comings and goings of air hostesses. Virginia Bruce and Jane Wyman played the pretty air hostesses, while tough pilots such as Dennis Morgan, Ralph Bellamy and Wayne Morris swarmed around them.

Also in 1940 came RKO's *MAN AGAINST THE SKY*, directed by Leslie Goodwins and starring Richard Dix, Edmund Lowe and Wendy Barrie.

Metro produced another exciting flying film in 1940 about a fighter squadron in the Navy. It was entitled *FLIGHT COMMAND* and was directed by Frank Borzage. Robert Taylor, Walter Pidgeon and Ruth Hussey appeared in the leading roles. The story was not perhaps the most original, but Borzage managed to make an exciting tale out of the development of an instrument landing system that could bring aircraft in to a safe landing in the fog.

A young flying cadet comes to the Navy's air arm in San Diego from Pensacola. He (Taylor) is arrogant and very much aware of his appeal to women. After a short time he becomes interested in the wife (Hussey) of the wing commander (Pidgeon). She in turn is not completely unresponsive. Her brother, who is also a pilot, is occupied with the construction of a landing system that will allow the pilots to land in the worst weather conditions, including fog. He tests his invention without being given permission, but something goes wrong with the machinery and he

All stills on next page are from Howard Hawks's ONLY ANGELS HAVE WINGS *from 1940.*
Top left: An airmail bird type Hamilton.
Top right: Cary Grant and Richard Barthelmess.
Below from left: Victor Killian, Lucio Villegas, Jean Arthur and Cary Grant. On the bed is Thomas Mitchell (dying). Behind, a glimpse of Pedro Regas and Pat Flaherty.

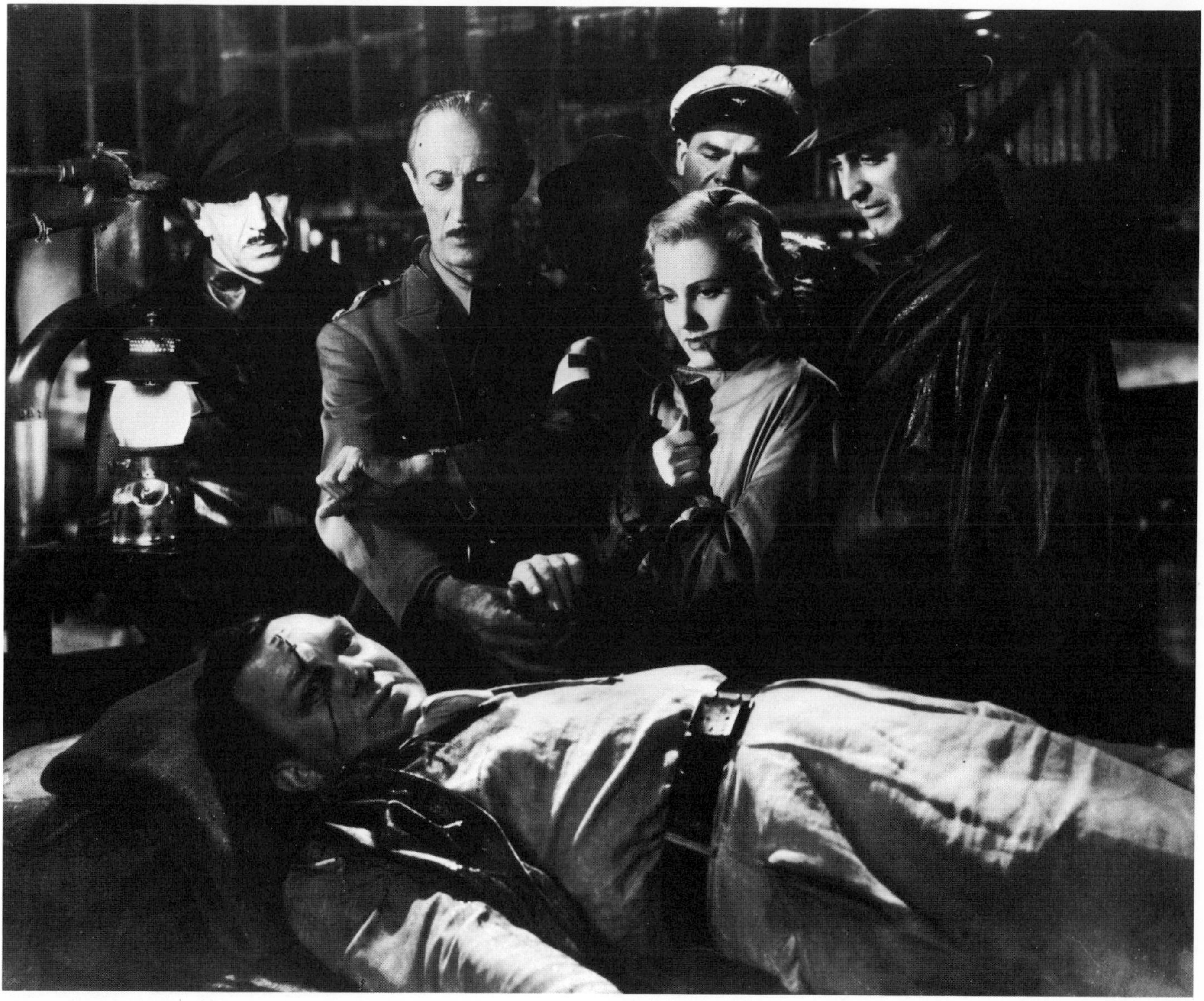

crashes and is killed. The sister is greatly upset by her brother's death, and she also now believes that she is in love with the new young pilot from Pensacola. The young man has made himself most unpopular by his pursuit of the wing commander's wife, but now he takes up her brother's unfinished invention and eventually succeeds in completing it. In addition to this, he saves his commander from crashing when the latter has run out of fuel.

The brilliant color photography, particularly in the flying sequences, helped to lift this above the standard level.

Metro Goldwyn Mayer presents ROBERT TAYLOR in Flight Command

"You've got me all wrong . . . I'm resigning, not quitting!"

COUNTRY OF ORIGIN U. S. A

Far left: George Brent (left) and John Payne in Lloyd Bacon's WINGS OF THE NAVY (1939). The model aircraft on the table is a Grumman F2F.

Near left: From the British documentary TARGET FOR TONIGHT (1941).

The great comedy team of Bud Abbott and Lou Costello shook up an American flight school in the 1940 release *KEEP 'EM FLYING.*

England also produced an air comedy in the early war years. George Formby was a kind, but incompetent, policeman who ended up in an R.A.F. uniform in *IT'S IN THE AIR* (1938). Part of the zany script was a "test flight" of a Hawker Hart type bomber.

In England the hardships of the Blitz were being overcome and in 1941 there was an excellent feature-length documentary produced. It was called *TARGET FOR TONIGHT,* and its creator, Harry Watt, by going along on a number of night raids over Germany, was able to provide the British with a highly authentic picture of the R.A.F. Bomber Command and its personnel.

The film followed the pilots through their briefing before taking off and then through the black night, out across the channel and over the enemy coastline to their target in Germany. It represented many hours of flying for the crews, and for the whole time enemy anti-aircraft fire and fighter planes made life on board a real hell. At last they pass over their targets for a few brief moments and then—home! In most cases the home base meant safety and rest. Unfortunately, not all of them returned to enjoy it.

By going in close on the faces of the crew of one of the planes—a Vickers Wellington with the code name *F for Freddie*—Watt gave the audience a chance to see the real men behind their oxygen masks and the tough outer facade they affected. He wished to show that they were not supermen but instead ordinary young men like anyone else, tense and frightened as they faced the unknown, the unknown that could end in a confrontation with death. But self-survival, team spirit and their sense of duty inspired the fortitude that was so essential.

TARGET FOR TONIGHT was made by the Crown Film Unit, which was in fact the film section of the Ministry of Defence. The purpose of the film was to use it as propaganda to strengthen the morale of the hard-pressed civilians, and as such it must be regarded as one of the very best films of its type made during the war. (In 1944 a similar American film was made called *MEMPHIS BELLE,* which will be dealt with later in this chapter.)

In *DANGEROUS MOONLIGHT,* Brian Desmond Hurst gave the filmgoer an exciting and romantic story of a Polish fighter pilot and concert pianist who escapes from

At left: Robert Taylor and Walter Pidgeon in Metro's FLIGHT COMMAND (1940).

Anton Walbrook and Derrick de Marney in DANGEROUS MOONLIGHT (1941).

burning Warsaw to England where he witnesses the blitz from the cockpit of an R.A.F. Spitfire. In this film Anton Walbrook played opposite Sally Gray, and the theme music, "The Warsaw Concerto" by Richard Addinsell, became famous.

In the early part of the war the R.A.F. received many reinforcements from North America and Canada. Much of this equipment was sent by ships in huge convoys, but there were also a number of aircraft flown over the Atlantic from Canada and the East Coast of the U.S. *INTERNATIONAL SQUADRON* (1941) was about the ferrying of these planes and starred Ronald Reagan and William Lundigan. It was produced by Warner Brothers and directed by Lewis Seiler. And, of course, on the ground there was a beautiful girl—Olympe Bradna.

Also in 1941 Paramount released two flying stories: *POWER DIVE* with Richard Arlen, Jean Parker and Roger Pryor, directed by James Hogan; then a really excellent film called *I WANTED WINGS,* by Mitchell Leisen. It was a well made and engaging film about flying training in the American Air Force. The pilots-to-be were played by Ray Milland, William Holden and Wayne Morris. Brian Donlevy played an instructor, and peek-a-boo beauty Veronica Lake also had a small role. It was an exciting film and provided straightforward propaganda for the Air Force—which was probably its purpose.

The United States was still not involved in

INTERNATIONAL SQUADRON (1941).

POWER DIVE (1941).

the war but the films of the time revealed clearly that it was rearming. More and more they were played against a military background and the final scenes often ended with mass demonstrations of military might manifested in both men and aircraft. An example is *DIVE BOMBER* (1941), made by Warners, with Errol Flynn in the lead as a doctor attached to the air arm of the Navy. It was an interesting film from a technical point of view, both as regards flying and problems in medicine, and dealt with the problem of acceleration stresses (gravitational force or "G") during steep turns and dives. In addition to this, the audience could also follow the development of pressurized flying suits and cabins for high altitude flying. The film was shot at the U.S. naval bases of Pensacola and

A North American NA-16 over Randolph Field in Arizona. From I WANTED WINGS (1941).

I WANTED WINGS (1941).

San Diego and on board the new aircraft carriers *Saratoga* and *Lexington*. There was a lot of beautiful flying in it. Among the aircraft was the small, stubby, tough Grumman F2F, a double-decked fighter. Also shown in the film were the two-engined Beechcraft and the powerful Vought-Sikorsky Vindicator—a beautiful dive-bomber that proved to be inadequate to its task when war broke out in December 1941. Flynn was assisted by Fred MacMurray, Ralph Bellamy, Regis Toomey and Alexis Smith. The film was directed by Michael Curtiz—perhaps Hollywood's very best creator of adventure films.

One of the climaxes of the film—there were a number—comes when Flynn makes an altitude flight test in one of the pressurized suits he himself has designed. Everyone knows that the suit has proved faulty earlier and the test flight is considered very dangerous. MacMurray, a test pilot who has previously shown scorn for Flynn's ideas and research, now changes his view. He has just learned that he has a weak heart and must give up flying. He tricks Flynn and replaces him in the cockpit of the small fighter plane in which the test is to be made. The takeoff goes well and he begins to climb to the test height of 40,000 feet. Soon the valves and tubes of the system that provide the flying suit with oxygen and pressure freeze up. Finally the life-giving oxygen is cut off completely and the unconscious MacMurray goes into his last dive. However, in his final mo-

ment of consciousness he succeeds in locating the fault in the system and writes down where it is on a notebook which is later found among the wreckage of the plane. In this way he conveys a message to his comrades that allows them to continue their research and tests, which in turn will enable future pilots to survive at very high altitudes.

The movie is also one of this author's favorites among films about flying. There are incredibly beautiful aerial shots in Technicolor and both the human and technical drama are very interesting.

In the same year Fox sent Tyrone Power to London to make *A YANK IN THE R.A.F.;* Betty Grable and John Sutton also appeared in it and the film was directed by Henry King. Also in that year, RKO produced a film about the British aviatrix Amy Johnson and her husband Jim Mollison. This one was en-

titled *THEY FLEW ALONE* and Miss Johnson was played by Anna Neagle.

Amy Johnson became famous through her flight to Australia in 1930. The film dealt largely with this flight and the one she made to America in 1933 together with her husband Jim Mollison (Robert Newton) in their plane called *Seafarer.* She later drowned in the Thames when she crash-landed in the river while ferrying an aircraft for the R.A.F.

The Royal Navy was also equipped with aircraft carriers, and *SHIPS WITH WINGS,* which had John Clements, Hugh Williams and Michael Wilding, was about fighter pi-

Far left: Regis Toomey is unconscious after a power dive. From Warner Bros.' DIVE BOMBER (1941).

Opposite page, top right: Robert Armstrong (left), Ralph Bellamy, Errol Flynn and Fred MacMurray in Michael Curtiz' "air medical" adventure DIVE BOMBER (1941).

Anna Neagle as the aviatrix Amy Johnson in THEY FLEW ALONE (1941). *The plane is a De Havilland DH 60 Moth.*

John Sutton and Tyrone Power as escaping partners in A YANK IN THE R.A.F. (1941).

Opposite page, below right: Herbert Anderson helps Fred MacMurray (left) with his pressure suit before the last test. The machine in the background is a Grumman F2F used in DIVE BOMBER (1941).

lots on board the *Ark Royal*—in 1941 the pride of the British fleet. Most of the action takes place in the Mediterranean and the denouement comes when John Clements, flying a Fairey Fulmar, sacrifices his life by crashing his aircraft into a dam that must be destroyed at all costs. A few good shots were taken in the air, but the majority of the dogfight and attacking scenes were shot with models of little verisimilitude. The film was directed by Sergei Nolbandov.

Universal's *FLYING CADETS* (1942) concerned flying training and in it Edmund Lowe, William Gargan and Peggy Moran were directed by Erle C. Kenton.

Pat O'Brien, Glenn Ford and Evelyn Keyes appeared in *FLIGHT LIEUTENANT* (1942),

produced by Columbia under the direction of Sidney Salkow. Basically it dealt with the same training program as the above-mentioned film and about the development of a new fighter plane. Originally it was given the title *HE'S MY OLD MAN*.

Warners' Michael Curtiz displayed his remarkable ability again in 1942 with *CAPTAINS OF THE CLOUDS*. This was about bush pilots in the vast wilderness of the Canadian North. They have much experience and many hours of flying behind them when they offer their services to the R.C.A.F. for the serious task of winning the war. Difficulties arise in the beginning but are soon straightened out, and Curtiz is able to direct one dramatic scene after another with some of Warners' top stars of the time—among whom were James Cagney, Dennis Morgan, Alan Hale, Reginald Gardiner and Brenda Marshall.

It was a pleasant film and filled with action. The high point comes when a squadron of Lockheed Hudsons is shown as it is ferried from Canada to England. The planes are unarmed and therefore cannot defend themselves when they are attacked by a German fighter. Cagney comes to the rescue to save his friends, sacrificing himself by ramming the German fighter with his plane and going down with it into the cold depths of the North Atlantic.

The Crown Film Unit, the film section of the Ministry of Defence, made a powerful

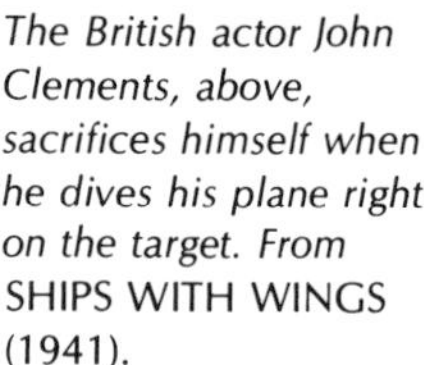

The British actor John Clements, above, sacrifices himself when he dives his plane right on the target. From SHIPS WITH WINGS (1941).

Far left: Pat O'Brien and Glenn Ford in FLIGHT LIEUTENANT (1942).

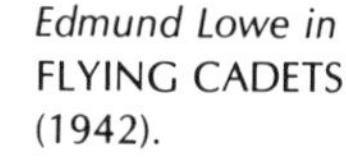

Edmund Lowe in FLYING CADETS (1942).

Next page, left: Three low level Hudsons in the British COASTAL COMMAND (1942).

Swedish poster of CAPTAINS OF THE CLOUDS (1942).

Bottom right: ONE OF OUR AIRCRAFT IS MISSING (1942). *The aircraft are Avro Lancasters.*

documentary in 1942 called *COASTAL COMMAND*. The director's name was J. B. Holmes and he made the film with the full cooperation of the R.A.F. and the Royal Navy. The film was about coastal reconnaissance and naval flying. The types of planes were mainly flying boats such as the Short Sunderland and Consolidated Catalina, and the search for U-boats took them over the North Atlantic and up to the great ice expanses of the sub-Arctic. The film is memorable for the realism it displayed in the depiction of this difficult and dangerous task.

Another film from England that year with a similar authenticity was *ONE OF OUR AIRCRAFT IS MISSING,* made by British National Films. It was a sort of semi-documentary, directed by Michael Powell and Emeric Pressburger. It was about Bomber Command and the enormous losses suffered during night raids over Germany. Appearing in it were Eric Portman and Hugh Williams.

Leslie Howard, the great British actor and director, was very personally committed to the battle against the enemy. His *PIMPERNEL SMITH* (1941) was and is an unforgettable and thrilling satire. In an early stage of his career, Hollywood too discovered him and so unfortunately he did not make many more films at home in England. Among these, however, we must mention *THE FIRST OF THE FEW* (1942), a film made in honor of the designer of the famous Supermarine Spitfire—Reginald J. Mitchell.

Mitchell's life story was related without disturbing glorification: from having begun

his career by designing locomotives he fought his way to the realization of his greatest dream—to build an airplane that was faster than any other. It was a long hard road, but through the building of the fast, beautiful seaplane Supermarine S-5 and S-6, which won the famous Schneider Cup competition, the idea gradually formed to design a high-speed, heavily armed fighter. Its origin was the experience gained with the above-mentioned seaplane.

The dream was realized in the Spitfire, which became perhaps the best-known aircraft in the world.

Leslie Howard played Mitchell and David Niven his good friend Crisp, a test pilot. Mitchell's wife was played by Rosamund John. The flying sequences in the film included some authentic footage of the Schneider Cup races. William Walton composed the "Spitfire Fugue" for the film, a dramatic piece of music in honor of the young pilots who fought and sacrificed their lives in the Battle of Britain.

Universal's *EAGLE SQUADRON* (1942) also dealt with Spitfire pilots and the R.A.F. It was an uneven movie about American volunteer pilots in the R.A.F. It was based on the fact that such a squadron existed, but of course the story was completely contrived. Robert Stack, Jon Hall and John Loder gave bravura performances as the fighter pilots and Diana Barrymore appeared as the sweet girlfriend. There were many action-filled air battles and Arthur Lubin managed to make the highpoint of the film almost nerve-shattering. The hero (Stack) has been given the task (between his duties as a fighter pilot) by the intelligence service of stealing a Messerschmitt. The point is to gain access to the latest German gunsight system. It goes without saying that he succeeds.

A separate sequel to this film was produced in 1948 under the title *FIGHTER SQUADRON*.

Errol Flynn was occasionally required to lay aside his sword and pistol and don a flying suit as in *DIVE BOMBER*. He did this again in 1942 under the direction of Raoul Walsh in *DESPERATE JOURNEY*. Actually it was not a genuine flying film but was closely related to the genre.

Leslie Howard as the aircraft designer R.J. Mitchell, here inspecting the first prototype of his Spitfire. From THE FIRST OF THE FEW (1942).

Flynn is skipper on an R.A.F. Flying Fortress. After completing a bombing mission over Germany, the plane is shot down and the survivors from the crew are forced to flee through enemy territory. The greater part of the film deals with their tribulations behind enemy lines. Finally they steal a German aircraft to complete their escape, leaving a trail of wreckage behind them, both in materiel and broken hearts. This was not one of Flynn's better films, despite the help given

Test pilot Crisp (Niven) pays Mitchell a visit shortly before he dies. From THE FIRST OF THE FEW (1942).

EAGLE SQUADRON (1942).

From left: Eddie Albert, Jon Hall, John Loder, Leif Erickson, Robert Stack and Edgar Barrier *in* EAGLE SQUADRON (1942).

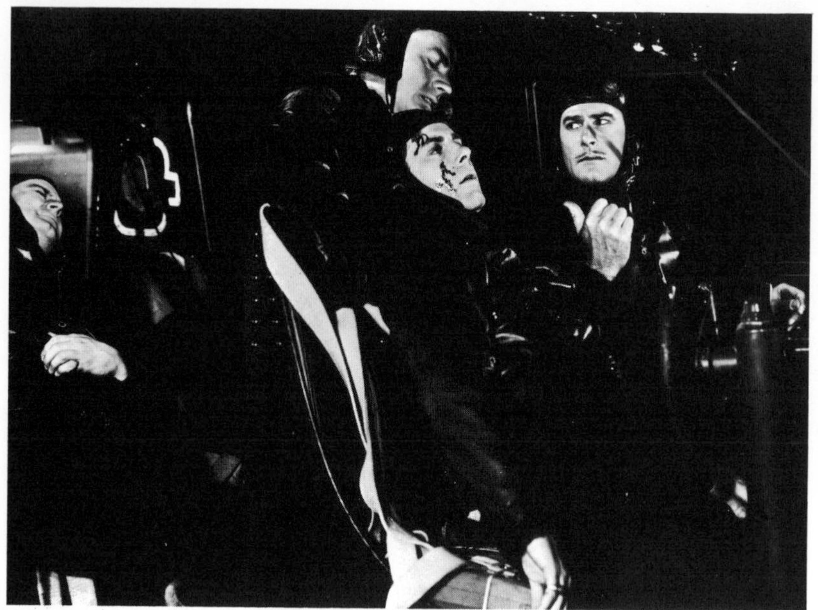

among many others were Amy Johnson, Amelia Earhart, Hanna Reich, Jacqueline Cochran, and Jacqueline Auriol. These were women who knew how an aircraft should be handled!

A few of them have had their lives portrayed on film. We have already mentioned *THEY FLEW ALONE* (1941) which told of the fate of Amy Johnson. In 1942 the time had come to tell the story of Amelia Earhart. In that year Lothar Mendes made *FLIGHT FOR FREEDOM* for RKO, with Rosalind Russell in the leading role which paralleled the life of the famous aviatrix. Amelia Earhart disappeared without a trace over the Pacific Ocean in 1937. At the time there was much wild speculation as to what happened to her, but a clear solution to the mystery was never

Warner Bros.' DESPERATE JOURNEY *(1942). From left: Arthur Kennedy, Patrick O'Moore (dying) and Errol Flynn.*

The photo in the center shows a squadron of AT-6 Texans. From THUNDER BIRDS *(1942).*

by Ronald Reagan, Arthur Kennedy and Alan Hale. Raymond Massey played a satanic German officer.

FLYING FORTRESS was made the same year and produced by the same company, Warners, using the same type of aircraft. Richard Greene played the lead and the film was directed by Walter Forde.

The theme of *THUNDER BIRDS* was about British pilots who received their training in the U.S. It was produced in 1942 and had Preston Foster, John Sutton and Gene Tierney in the leading roles. The American flying instructor (Foster) and the British student pilot (Sutton) are rivals for the affections of an American girl (Tierney). Problems develop both in the flying training and the love affair. Beautiful flying scenes alternate with more problems and more romance until a happy end is reached at last.

After an almost ageless battle for equality, women of today have finally, at least in some parts of the world, achieved a fair degree of equality with men. But for a long time now it has been shown—in fact since the beginning of time—that women were capable of standing on their own two feet. How did Eve manage in the Garden of Eden? All right, no one knows for sure—but in the "typically masculine" world of flying there have always been a number of "tough birds." Famous

found. In the film, the male lead was taken by Fred MacMurray. It was not a bad film, over-romanticized of course, but still rather interesting.

The training and job of air gunner were well described in *AERIAL GUNNER* (1943), directed by William H. Pine for Paramount, starring Richard Arlen, Chester Morris and Jimmy Lydon. It was a rather thin story, but not completely uninteresting as a flying film with plenty of action.

SQUADRON LEADER X, produced by RKO in 1943, concerned a German flying

Top left: AERIAL GUNNER (1943).

Top right: Rosalind Russell and Herbert Marshall in the story of Amelia Earhart— FLIGHT FOR FREEDOM (1943).

Below right: Richard Greene (left) in Walter Forde's FLYING FORTRESS (1942).

officer (Eric Portman) who nested in the R.A.F. as a pilot. In actual fact, he was a spy. Ann Dvorak represented the distaff side in this fairly exciting but otherwise uninteresting thriller directed by Lance Comfort.

In 1942 William Wyler was awarded an Oscar for *MRS. MINIVER*. This was the last film he made before he left the film factory and entered the war service. However, in 1944 he made a feature-length documentary film for the Department of Defence entitled *THE MEMPHIS BELLE*. This told the story of the crew of a B-17 Flying Fortress participating in daylight raids over Germany in 1943. This was during a period in the war when aircraft losses were truly enormous. Wyler himself and his photographer William Clothier went along on a number of actual raids. They were well stocked with cameras and color film and the final result was little short of fantastic. *MEMPHIS BELLE,* like the British *TARGET FOR TONIGHT,* must be ranked among the very best documentaries ever made about flying.

In this film Wyler and Clothier had managed to capture the fantastic experience of flying, in color and in a most dramatic fashion. Certainly it was the war itself that formed the background, but the beauty of the sky and clouds and free space and adventure could not be denied. One beautiful scene after another unfolded on the screen as the great bomber armada headed for its target, in this case Wilhelmshaven. The vapor trails were like chalk lines in the sky above Europe and the escorting fighters flashed past like silver confetti.

But then everything changes. The exploding shells of the anti-aircraft fire burst in flower-like patterns and the detonations increase in density. Enemy fighter planes attack from all angles, with the intention of killing. One bomber after another is seen to burst in flames or explode into pieces. There is nothing very romantic about this, and the movie viewer sitting comfortably in his seat

Eric Portman in SQUADRON LEADER X (1943).

A Flying Fortress somewhere above Europe. A scene from William Wyler's documentary masterpiece THE MEMPHIS BELLE (1944).

They flew her all the twenty-five tours to hell and back—this is the real crew of THE MEMPHIS BELLE. *From left: Harold P. Lock, Cecil H. Scott, Robert J. Hanson, James A. Varinis, Robert K. Morgan (captain), Charles B. Leighton, John P. Quinlan, Casimer A. Nastal, Vincent R. Evans and Clarence E. Winchell.*

suddenly feels the reality of war disturbingly close. The cold sweat and tension on the actor's faces become contagious.

Wyler and Clothier were along on *Memphis Belle*'s last raid, completing the tour of duty that included twenty-five bombing missions, and they were lucky in using this particular plane for their camera platform. Many other planes failed to return even from their first mission.

It is interesting to note that the *Memphis Belle* later flew an additional tour of duty and after these twenty-five raids she was "pensioned off." She had never been severely damaged and received only a few "minor wounds" during the whole of her service.

In 1944 Wyler also was commissioned by the U.S. Navy to make another documentary. This was entitled *THE FIGHTING LADY* and was about naval operations in the Pacific and aircraft carriers and their crews. The reader will find out more about this film in the next chapter.

The bombers, at right, on to their way toward the target—Germany. From THE MEMPHIS BELLE (1944).

George Cukor told about the training of fighter pilots in Fox's *WINGED VICTORY,* a good, straight story about flying, well photographed and with attractive actors such as Lon McCallister, Edmond O'Brien, Gary Merrill and Don Taylor in the main roles. Their days were gilded by the presence of Jeanne Crain.

In 1945 some filmmakers abruptly returned to the "glorious war of 1918." Lloyd Bacon made *CAPTAIN EDDIE,* with Fred MacMurray playing the title role as Eddie Rickenbacker. Other performers included Charles Bickford, Lloyd Nolan, Lynn Bari and James Gleason.

Perhaps the best film about flying ever made in England was produced in 1945. It was called *THE WAY TO THE STARS* and in the cast were John Mills, Rosamund John, Michael Redgrave and Douglass Montgomery. Anthony Asquith, one of the United Kingdom's greatest directors, made it, and the screenplay was written by Terence Rattigan. The film was about a group of British and American flyers at a base somewhere in England. We were able to watch the unfolding of their lives, their loves, and their deaths.

From left: Don Taylor, Barry Nelson, Edmond O'Brien, Rune Hultman, Mark Daniels and Lon McCallister in WINGED VICTORY (1944).

The film opened with a long tracking shot over the deserted and decrepit airfield. In rapid flashbacks the audience is taken back to the hectic war years of 1940—an idea that was used by Henry King a few years later in *TWELVE O'CLOCK HIGH*.

Two pilots, Peter and David (John Mills and Michael Redgrave), become close friends. Peter is carrying on a love affair with a young woman (Renée Asherson) but refuses to marry her after his friend has been killed. David has left a wife (Rosamund John) and small child. Some American pilots arrive at the base as reinforcements. In the beginning there occur a number of misunderstandings which cause bad blood between the Americans and their British colleagues, but eventually these are ironed out and a strong bond of friendship develops. Finally Peter returns to his girl and the grim daily game of war goes on.

Asquith and Rattigan had captured beautifully the daily life of the pilots and the internecine conflict between the two very different types of men—"I'm an American, you're only English." Much of *THE WAY TO THE STARS* may seem passé and antiquated today, but many of the views expressed still hold up very well. Brilliant performances by everybody in it helped to raise this film to the very highest level in the genre.

Richard Attenborough played opposite Edward G. Robinson in *JOURNEY TOGETHER* (1945). Aside from a few professional actors, including Robinson, borrowed from Hollywood to film for a few weeks in England, all the other men appearing in the movie were members of the R.A.F., R.C.A.F. and the U.S. Army Air Force.

The film, which was more or less a semi-documentary, was directed by John Boulting and told the story of two young pilots being trained for the R.A.F. and their subsequent experiences as fighter pilots. Oddly enough this film, for once, did not treat the two young men as rivals for the affections of a pretty young girl. In fact, there were no romantic sequences in the film at all. Unless one includes the love of flying.

From left: Michael Redgrave, Trevor Howard and John Mills in THE WAY TO THE STARS (1945).

Below left: Richard Attenborough, Jack Watling and Edward G. Robinson in JOURNEY TOGETHER (1945).

Below: Douglass Montgomery as one of the American airmen in THE WAY TO THE STARS (1945).

A Swedish poster of THE WAY TO THE STARS (1945).

The two men, played by Attenborough and Jack Watling, are going through their flying training. One of them (Attenborough) is not able to meet all the requirements and is "washed out." But then he allows himself to be talked into taking a navigational course instead. His disappointment is, of course, enormous, but he soon learns that the navigator can sometimes be more important on board a bomber than the more glamorous pilot.

The film had a wonderful dénouement in an expertly photographed sequence of a bombing raid over the burning Berlin. Attenborough and Watling both gave convincing performances, and Edward G. Robinson was sympathetic as the flying instructor at a base in Arizona. As a whole, it was a good journeyman job of filmmaking about the daily life of flyers and the psychological stresses they operated under in battle.

In 1945 Michael Powell and Emeric Pressburger made a rather unusual film which bore some associations with flying. It was called *A MATTER OF LIFE AND DEATH* and had an excellent cast that included David Niven, Roger Livesey, Kim Hunter and Raymond Massey. It concerns a young bomber pilot (Niven) who, on the return flight from a raid, is forced to leave his burning Lancaster in midflight when the rest of his crew have been killed. The problem is that he is forced to jump without his parachute. Because of the fire on board he is unable to reach it and prefers to jump without it rather than die by fire. He plunges from a great height, but destiny has him fall into the sea and he is eventually washed up on a sandy beach.

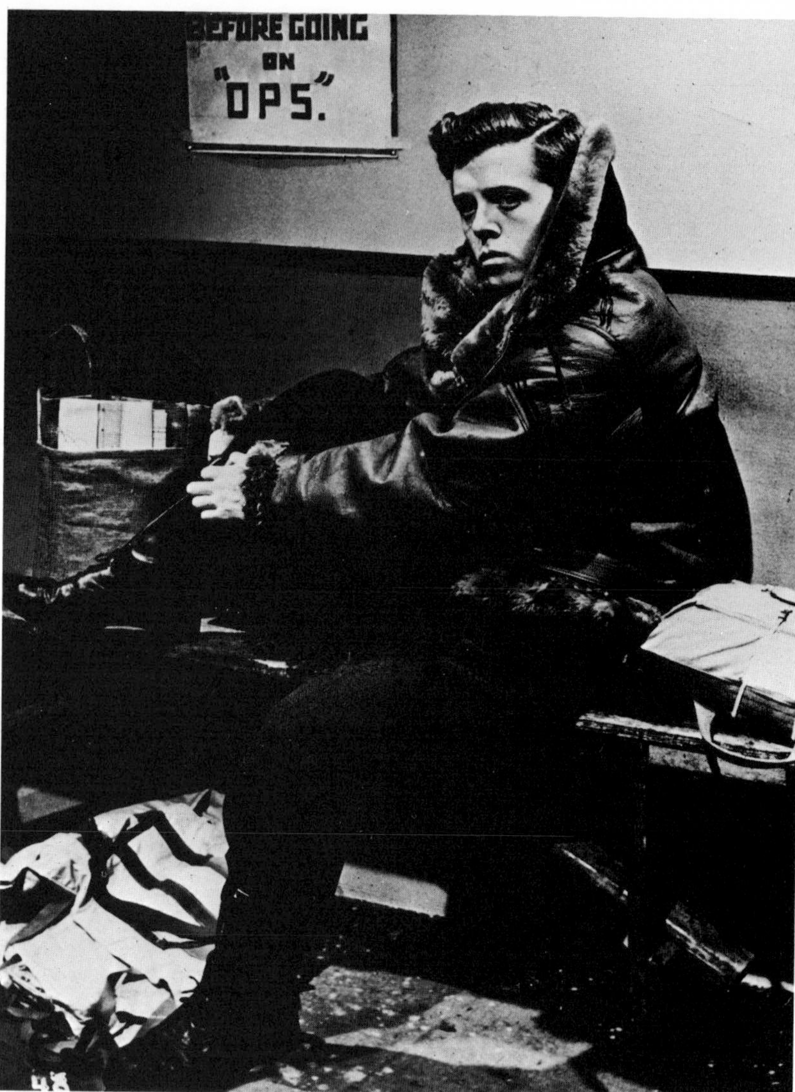

Richard Attenborough as the navigator in JOURNEY TOGETHER (1945).

He lies unconscious on the shore while his case is dealt with "up above" in the highest of all courts. The question is whether he should be struck off the rolls or whether he should be given another chance to live.

He is brought before the divine Judge and is given a defending counsel (Livesey) who turns out to be a friend indeed, while back on earth there is a young girl (Hunter) at operational headquarters who has fallen in love with him.

There is a long drawn-out "trial" before he is finally acquitted and allowed to remain

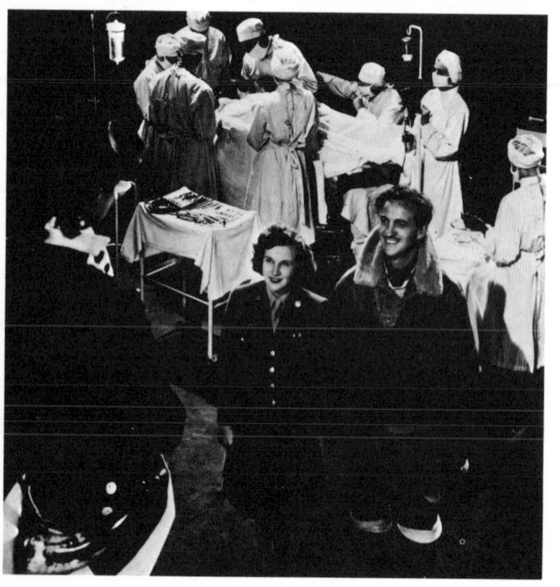

David Niven and Kim Hunter in A MATTER OF LIFE AND DEATH (1945).

Glenn Ford (as John J. Montgomery) and Janet Blair in William Wellman's GALLANT JOURNEY (1946).

Ouch! From GALLANT JOURNEY (1946).

on earth. Then love blossoms between the two young people and it all ends happily.

If this last film was somewhat outside the framework of this anthology, then the next one most certainly belongs within it. It is about one of America's very first flyers (no, as a matter of fact, the Wright Brothers were not the first) and is entitled *GALLANT JOURNEY*. In it Glenn Ford played John J. Montgomery, a pioneer pilot who flew for the first time in 1883 in a glider. He died quite young in a similar flight when he was carrying out some rather advanced tests. It was a rather interesting story and directed with tireless enthusiasm by William A. Wellman. A number of Montgomery's own airplanes were specially constructed for the production from the original plans. Janet Blair and Charlie Ruggles played two important roles in the film, made in 1946 by Columbia.

In *BLAZE OF NOON* (1947), Paramount produced a story of mail pilots in the wild Sierra mountains. Under the direction of John Farrow, Sterling Hayden, William Holden and William Bendix flew small rickety aircraft that were little more than flying coffins. But these pilots continued to carry the post, partly because they loved danger and flying and partly because this was how they made their living. Naturally love was not far off, in the beautiful feminine apparition of Anne Baxter. Two tough younger pilots were played by Sonny Tufts and Johnny Sands.

During 1943–44, the United States sent its best fighter planes to Europe to escort its bomber squadrons on their daylight raids over Germany's industrial areas, and they even flew as far as Berlin. Mainly these aircraft were the P-51 Mustang and the P-47 Thunderbolt, both long-range fighters. American bomber pilots no longer needed to feel alone over enemy territory. They could count

BLAZE OF NOON (1947). *The plane is a Pitciern.*

Fred MacMurray as Eddie Rickenbacker, one of the greatest air heroes of WWI. From CAPTAIN EDDIE (1945).

ring
NNE BAXTER
ILLIAM HOLDEN
ONNY TUFTS
ILLIAM BENDIX
ERLING HAYDEN
Howard Da Silva · Johnny Sands
Wallace · Edith King
uced by Robert Fellows
cted by JOHN FARROW
enplay by Frank Wead and
r Sheekman
ramount Re-Release

From left: William Holden, Anne Baxter and Sterling Hayden in BLAZE OF NOON (1947).

FIGHTER SQUADRON (1948).

on help when attacked by German fighters now.

FIGHTER SQUADRON (1948) was a film about just such a squadron, equipped with P-47s. In a way it was a kind of sequel to *EAGLE SQUADRON* (1942). The action took place in the same squadron and the leading role was taken by Robert Stack, who played the same character in the earlier film. Warner Brothers had Raoul Walsh direct the film, which guaranteed that it would have plenty of speed and action-filled escapes! In fact, one of the more exciting episodes was an escape—of a rather unusual kind.

The squadron leader (Edmond O'Brien) is hit and his plane catches fire. He has to parachute to safety. He lands in a French field and is spotted by a German patrol. A wild chase ensues. One of the group commanders in the squadron (Stack) saw his leader jump and has located the spot where he landed. He finds a suitable glade to bring his own plane down in and manages to land very near his hotly pursued friend. Parachute and other nonessential equipment are thrown out of the plane and both men jam themselves into the single-seat aircraft, give it full throttle and take off right in front of the wildly gesticulating Germans. It was a lively sequence and would seem a most unlikely turn of events, but it appears that such an exploit was actually carried out by some mad pilot during the war. There was little depth to the characterizations in the film although certain personal conflicts added something. But it was a good straightforward flying film and many of the subordinate roles were well played by such actors as John Rodney and Henry Hull.

Some very good movies about the so-called "decision makers"—those who had the ultimate responsibility for people and events in the great machinery of war—were also produced during the latter part of the forties.

One of these was released in 1948, directed by Sam Wood and titled *COMMAND DECISION*. Wood had practically the whole action of the film take place in a single location—the headquarters of Strategic Bomber Command in England. The film dealt with the period in the war when the Americans had commenced their great raids over central Germany, a time of great losses in both men and aircraft. The way the story unfolds gives the film something of the quality of a psychological drama.

The fact that there were hardly any aircraft or flying scenes in the film was not particularly disturbing, although for those people who expected to see a lot of action and flying it must have been something of a disappointment. There were a few shots of bombing raids over the "Fatherland" and a few scenes of the planes landing as they returned to their bases. There were, in fact, a couple of good authentic crash landings. Clark Gable gave a powerful performance as a general when, from the headquarters, he attempted to "talk down" a severely injured pilot. The other generals and colonels composing the brain trust were portrayed by a group of some of the best known stars of the forties. In addition to Clark Gable, Metro had a cast that included Walter Pidgeon, Van Johnson, Charles Bickford, John Hodiak and Brian Donlevy.

This picture showed that filmmakers had at last gained a more mature and intelligent view of the war and its effects. Fox displayed this same intelligence once more in 1949 with Henry King's *TWELVE O'CLOCK HIGH*. The title is Air Force jargon for "straight ahead, over!" or "we are right over the target!"

The main theme was still the daylight raids over the Ruhr Valley, Bremen, Hamburg and Berlin. But there was no longer any attempt at glorification of the crews and individual characters. Now there was an emphasis on the tremendous psychological pressure brought about by fear, tension, and hope, all of which were experienced during these raids by everyone from the ranking officers to the lowliest aircraftsman.

In *COMMAND DECISION* we were able to follow the actions of those who made the decisions, the men with the brilliant minds who planned the raids that had to be carried out, all with a single purpose—*to end the war, to win it!* In Henry King's film we could meet the men who did the job—flyers who made the journey to hell and back two or three times a week. Many of them, far too many, had only a one-way ticket.

Robert Stack picks his buddy (Edmond O'Brien) up into the cockpit of his P-47. From FIGHTER SQUADRON (1948).

The central character in *TWELVE O'CLOCK HIGH* was Brigadier General Savage, excellently portrayed by Gregory Peck. This film figure had a real-life counterpart in Major General Frank A. Armstrong who led the first daylight raids over Germany.

The structure of the story is built with flashbacks (as in *THE WAY TO THE STARS*). The person who recalls it all is Savage's former adjutant, Major Stovell, played by Dean Jagger with such skill that he was awarded an Oscar for the best male supporting role in 1949. Stovell comes to London a few

Clark Gable and John Hodiak in the MGM drama COMMAND DECISION (1948).

Above, from left: Hugh Marlowe, Dean Jagger, Gregory Peck and Gary Merrill in the high tension drama TWELVE O'CLOCK HIGH (1949).

A Martin T4M over the giant aircraft carrier Saratoga *in Warner Bros.'* TASK FORCE (1949).

Edmond O'Brien in FIGHTER SQUADRON (1948).

years after the war is over and goes out to the airfield which was the base of the 918th Bomber Wing at the time of the air raids. The field is now deserted and overgrown with weeds, but as he stands there and lets his eyes sweep over the decaying barracks and sees how the cracked asphalt runway is disappearing under the wild vegetation, he relives once again the events of the war years. The roar of plane engines is heard and he recalls the hectic days when Savage first arrived at the base to take over from the previous commander, Colonel Davenport (Gary Merrill). This latter had had a nervous breakdown and was temporarily relieved of his duties.

Savage makes himself unpopular within the first few days by his punctiliousness and near fanatical zeal. But before long the squadron learns that the new commander is a veritable rock of stability. His planning of the raids against the heavily defended industrial areas of Germany is masterful and

From left: John Ridgely, Bruce Bennett and Gary Cooper. Aircraft behind is a Douglas Dauntless. From the Warner film TASK FORCE (1949).

he leads the squadron with determination. He provides the essential support for raising the morale, which is much needed, since even the bravest among them suffers fear.

Savage, too, eventually reaches the point where psychologically and morally the human mechanism can stand no more. He has become more and more involved personally in the fate of the men he leads. His inclination is to protect them and he feels a growing reluctance—indeed an aversion—to the idea of sending them on missions that he knows will mean death for many of them. Finally he too breaks down and must be physically prevented from taking off with his men on the dangerous raids that he must, as commander, order his crews to execute.

Gregory Peck has said that he regards this as one of his best performances, and he is certainly right. Fox invested a great deal in this film. They cast their best actors, used their best director and photographer, the music was first-rate, and the final result met all their expectations—a great film, one of the greatest films about flying ever made.

Yet another worthwhile film was made in 1949. This was entitled *TASK FORCE,* with Gary Cooper, Walter Brennan, Wayne Morris and Jane Wyatt. Directed by Delmer Daves, it was about the development of the U.S. Navy's own special aircraft. It also portrayed the rise of the aircraft carrier to a position of great strategic importance—the Army and the government had generally regarded its development as "absurd."

The film included authentic and unique material from an earlier time and in the final stages of the Pacific war changed from black and white to spectacular color. In actual fact, it included much color film taken and preserved from the operations at Midway, Leyte and the Coral Sea, to name only a few of the battle areas where, in the early forties, the horizon seemed to be on fire.

Once again we are on the threshold of a new decade. Almost five years have passed since the peace agreement was signed, and actually consideration of the films made during the Second World War should end here, but there is still a section of the globe that we have not yet visited—the Pacific Ocean with its gigantic archipelago of islands. We have already mentioned briefly the great battles that were fought there between 1941 and 1945, but they also formed the background to a large number of other films of varying interest, and we come to these in the next section of this chapter.

Gregory Peck in his very convincing portrait of General Savage in TWELVE O'CLOCK HIGH (1949).

Against the Rising Sun

When the Japanese attacked the American naval base of Pearl Harbor in the Hawaiian Islands on December 7, 1941, they did so without first declaring war. In the jargon of politics this is called a sneak attack, and it certainly was all of that. History tells us that the greater part of the American fleet went to the bottom. Only a very few planes of the small fleet of aircraft stationed on the base managed to get into the air. And those that did were shot out of the sky like sparrows. The aircraft that could perhaps have done some good were far away at the time of the attack, as luck would have it, on board aircraft carriers that were out on maneuvers. Luck in the sense that these were virtually the only ships that the Navy had left to carry on hostilities against the new enemy. They were also perhaps the most important ships, giants of the sea which would form the basis of a whole new type of marine warfare—sea battles with airplanes.

Pearl Harbor was quickly turned into an inferno by the daring Japanese pilots, and this event has been shown many times on film with documentary sequences from the actual attack. Unquestionably these scenes give a clear picture of the progress of the action. From the Japanese point of view it was a completely successful operation, carried out by the Imperial Japanese Navy and its carrier-based aircraft.

Those films that were made, primarily in the United States, but also in Japan, during the four years that the Pacific war lasted, dealt largely with the air war carried out on the carrier-based fleets of aircraft belonging to the U.S. Navy and Marines.

But let us begin in the proper place—in the country that started the war in the Pacific.

Just prior to the outbreak of war, Japan produced a great many films, among which were a number of exceptional war movies. Film researchers have known about them but no prints have been available. Quite recently, however, a few well-preserved copies have been discovered of, among others, *FIVE SCOUTS* made in 1938 and directed by Tomotaka Tasaka. For the time this particular film was remarkably pacifistic, and it was also a good film. This type of movie was soon banned by the Japanese government. If war films were to be made, they would have to be nationalistic.

In 1940 Yutaka Abe made a flying film in accordance with this condition. He was one of the leading directors in Japan and was especially interested in making films dealing with flying. It was called *THE BURNING SKY* and showed for the first time in Japanese history a large amount of authentic aerial photography.

Another director of similar caliber to Abe was Kajiro Yamamoto who made *NIPPON'S YOUNG EAGLES* in 1941, a copy of which was sent to Hitler to underline the German/Japanese alliance. Yamamoto's film was about the training and heroism of the young Japanese pilots. Japanese soldiers have always been known for their near fanatical zeal and willingness to sacrifice themselves, and these military pilots were no exception. In a later stage in the war the essence of fanaticism and self-sacrifice was reached in the terrifying suicidal actions of the Kamikaze pilots—"the flyers of the divine wind."

In 1942 Yamamoto also made *SOUTH SEAS BOUQUET* and the epic, *THE WAR AT SEA FROM HAWAII TO MALAYA*. The latter was a story in praise of the Japanese Navy and its flyers, who are extravagantly honored as the film culminates in the attack on Pearl Harbor. This was awarded the prize as the best film of the year in Japan.

The subject of flying interested Eiichi Koishi, too, and in 1941 he directed *THE SOARING PASSION,* a semi-documentary sailplane story. And in 1944 the same director made *GENERAL KATO'S FALCON FIGHTERS*.

A very popular movie about flying cadets was directed in 1943 by Kunio Watanabe. It was called *TOWARDS THE DECISIVE BATTLE IN THE SKY*. With *NAVY* (1943), Tomotaka Tasaka contributed greatly to the further glorification of the pilots who bombed Pearl Harbor. After 1944 there were no more films about flying made in Japan.

The landing signals officer takes care of his buddies when they come back from their mission. From William Wyler's THE FIGHTING LADY (1944).

There were many other war movies in which flying sequences were integrated into the overall action. *THE DIVINE SOLDIERS OF THE SKY* was a typical propaganda documentary made in 1942 in honor of Japanese paratroops.

In 1945 the war ended for the island empire in the Pacific. We know now that it was the atomic bombs dropped over Hiroshima and Nagasaki which finally brought this country's fanatical soldiers to their knees.

In 1956, however, Hiroshi Noguschi directed a war film called *WEEP, PEOPLE OF JAPAN—THE LAST PURSUIT PLANE,* and as late as 1961–62 there were two films from Japan on the subject that was believed to be forgotten.

The first was called *THE ZERO FIGHTER* and told about that most famous weapon of the Japanese Air Force, the Mitsubishi A6M Zero fighter plane. This air story was directed by Toshio Masuda and must be described as representing a kind of awful nostalgia.

The second film was entitled *A STORM FROM THE SEA* (1961) and, under the direction of Shue Matsubayashi, showed everything that had been shown earlier in Japanese and Western films so often: the attack on Pearl Harbor. The attack was revived once again with the aid of unbelievably bad models mixed with documentary material and newly filmed sequences.

On the other hand, Matsubayashi did succeed in creating a fairly interesting if gruesome tale about the greatly feared suicide pilots who entered the Pacific war during its final, desperate phase. This film was called *WINGS OF THE SEA* and was made in 1962. And with this let us finish with "the soldiers of the divine wind" and their progress across the silver screen.

One can follow the participation of the United States in the Pacific war through many Hollywood productions, and for those in search of war films from the period we recommend Clyde Jeavons' book *A Pictorial History of War Films,* which is a rich source of information.

In a description of these particular war films, I feel that it is appropriate to begin with the Japanese war against China in 1940.

FLYING TIGERS (1942), directed by David Miller and starring John Wayne, John Carroll and Paul Kelly, concerned a handful of American volunteer pilots who fought in a flying corps formed and commanded by General Claire Chennault. It was called the A.V.G. (American Voluntary Group) and it fought Chiang Kai-Shek against the Japanese Air Force. The force was equipped with Curtiss P-40s, a fighter in which the pilots confronted the fast, new, highly maneuverable Mitsubishi Zero. At the time, the Japanese Air Force was very well equipped. It possessed a number of advanced bombers already in service and other new fighters were being tested or were well into the late planning stage: The Zero proved to be an excellent fighter and was much more easily maneuvered and more suitable for dogfights

Top: A scene from the Japanese film THE WAR AT SEA FROM HAWAII TO MALAYA (1942). *It shows a Nakajima B5N2 Kate taking off prepared for an attack against Pearl Harbor.*

Lower photo from the 1942 film shows the bridge of the Agaki, flagship of the Japanese carrier fleet. It was later sunk at the Battle of the Midway.

Facing page: A scene from the Japanese film A STORM FROM THE SEA (1962). *Actor in foreground is Toshiro Mifune.*

From left: Paul Kelly, John Wayne, Anna Lee and John Carroll in FLYING TIGERS (1942).

than the heavy Curtiss aircraft. But since the American pilots were better trained they succeeded in getting the upper hand over their enemy and to a great extent were able to protect the Chinese population from the terror bombing resorted to by the Japanese.

As a matter of fact, David Miller succeeded in creating an exciting and fairly accurate picture of the situation against a really authentic background. Wayne gave his usual rather wooden, bluff performance as a squadron commander who receives a couple of new recruits into the squadron. One of them is a little over-age (Kelly) and has difficulty in judging distances accurately. The other (Carroll) is really a mad adventurer who flies like the devil himself. After a time Wayne finds it necessary to restrain him and he is prohibited from flying. In an air battle Kelly misjudges the distance from another plane and crashes into it, and so, since pilots are needed, Wayne takes Carroll along with him on a rather primitive bombing raid in an old converted Boeing 247 passenger plane. This trip ends as one would expect. The aircraft runs into trouble on its approach to target and when it has been badly hit they decide to abandon it. Our adventurer tricks Wayne into parachuting from the plane first—with a helping push—and then he himself returns to the controls. In a last desperate attempt to complete the bombing attack he crashes on the target. He succeeds in his mission, but sacrifices his life.

A model scene showing a Mitsubishi Zero attacking U.S. Navy ships at Pearl Harbor. From the Japanese film A STORM FROM THE SEA (1962).

Before the house lights go up again, Wayne is reunited with the woman who has remained more or less in the background throughout the film—played by Anna Lee.

In 1943, RKO produced *BOMBARDIER* with Randolph Scott, Pat O'Brien, Anne Shirley and Robert Ryan. Once again it was about bombing raids, under the direction of Richard Wallace. Not a great film, but there was much good aerial photography and some drama.

One of the really big ones among feature films from the war was made in 1943 by Howard Hawks for Warner Bros. Its title was *AIR FORCE,* a wonderful film that deserves a place among the very greatest.

The story was based on a real situation. In 1941 a squadron of Flying Fortresses were to transfer their base of operations from California to Honolulu in Hawaii. The squadron was led by Major R. H. Carmichael and Lieutenant B. Allen.

When they arrived at their destination on December 7, all hell had broken loose. Hickam Field, where they were to land, and other adjoining fields and the naval base of Pearl Harbor were in a state of complete chaos. Everything had been wrecked by the Japanese attack.

It is against this background that Hawks builds his film. After the exceptionally exciting opening as the bombers arrive at Hawaii, we follow the adventures and fate of a single aircraft. The name of the plane is *Mary Ann* and its skipper is Captain Quincannon (John Ridgely). He succeeds in flying his aircraft to Manila via Wake Island where he picks up a stranded fighter pilot as a passenger.

In Manila they are attacked by the Japanese and the plane is damaged. After many tribulations they manage to repair her and then head for Australia. But first they have to carry out an attack on the Japanese Navy. This they do, but are then themselves attacked by enemy fighters. The plane is severely damaged and Quincannon seriously wounded. They have trouble as they try to return to their base and finally Quincannon gives the order to abandon the aircraft. They all parachute out except for one man, Winocki (John Garfield). He is the gunner on board but has also been trained as a pilot—he was washed out of the course before graduation. He takes over the controls and succeeds in flying the damaged plane and the wounded skipper back to the base in Manila.

The crew is reunited at Clark Field outside Manila, which is under enemy attack. Quincannon dies, but the passenger, Lieutenant

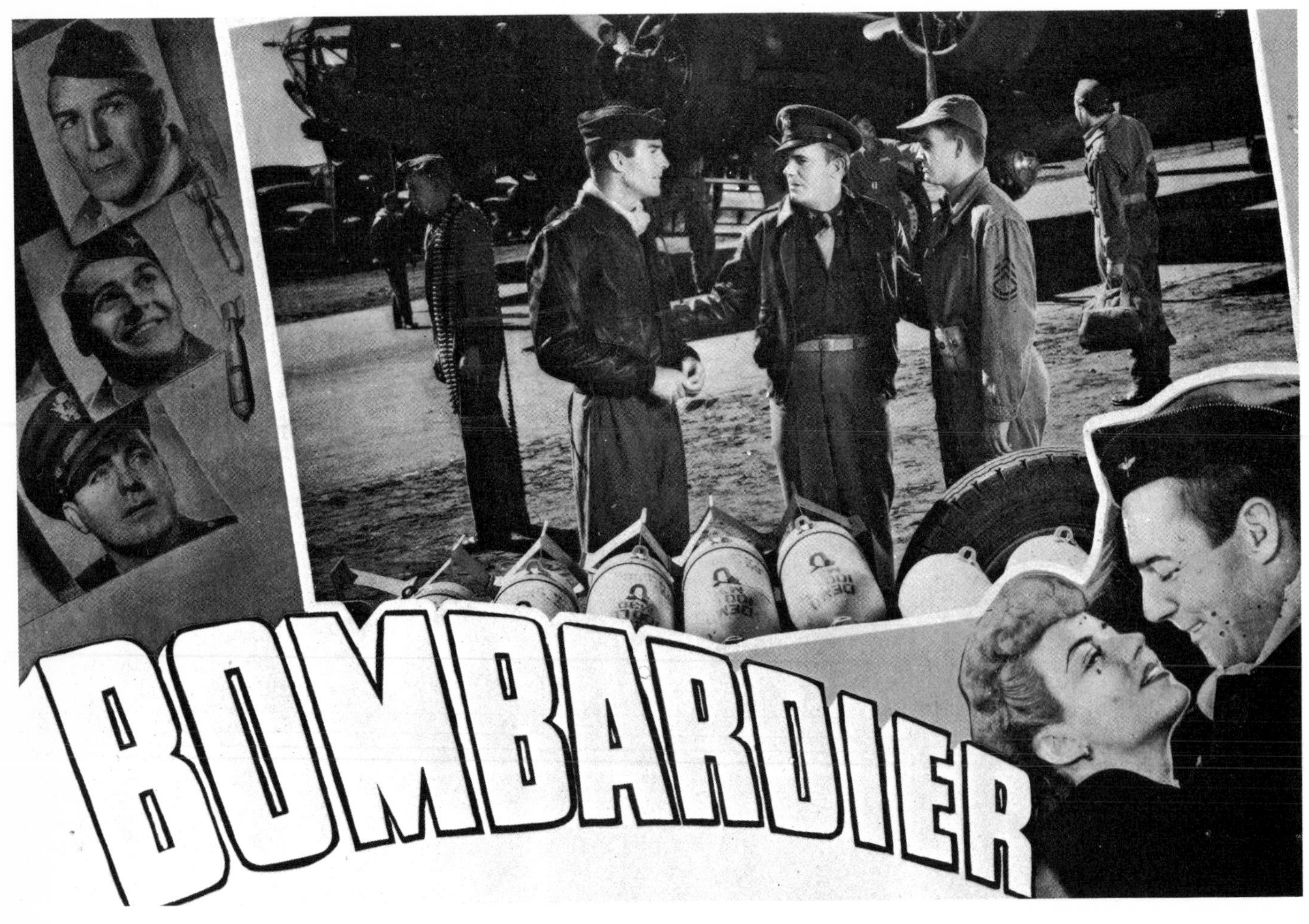

BOMBARDIER (1943).

*A Flying Fortress somewhere on a jungle strip. From the direct hit of Howard Hawks—*AIR FORCE (1943).

Rader, takes over command and flies the plane and its crew away from the battle of the Philippines. They set course for Australia and on the way become involved in the battle of the Coral Sea. On its arrival in Australia the *Mary Ann* crash-lands and burns up. The crew escapes uninjured, however, and are given another aircraft to carry on the fight; they name her *Mary Ann II*.

In *AIR FORCE* John Garfield performed one of his greatest character roles and received excellent support from his comrades Gig Young (second pilot), Arthur Kennedy (bombardier), Charles Drake (navigator) and James Brown as Lieutenant Rader.

John Garfield as Sergeant Winocki in AIR FORCE (1943).

AIR FORCE is one of this author's all-time favorites, and the beautifully controlled direction of Howard Hawks must, without exaggeration, make it one of the real classics.

In the same year (1943) Metro released two acceptable flying films—*PILOT 5,* directed by George Sidney, and *A GUY NAMED JOE* by Victor Fleming.

The first of these was perhaps the most interesting for anyone who cares about flying. In this film the famous P-38 was shown for the first time. The unconventional Lockheed Lightning was already well known by reputation and the USAAF succeeded, largely because of this aircraft, in getting the upper hand in air battles in which it was used—with, of course, the invaluable help of the naval and marine Corsairs and Hellcats.

Aside from the purely flying/technical aspects, *A GUY NAMED JOE* was the story of a gang of young fighter pilots belonging to a fighter wing somewhere in the Pacific. One of them was played by Van Johnson who, after his recent breakthrough in *Dr. Gillespie's New Assistant* (1942), was now ranked as one of Metro's newest stars.

The commander of the squadron was played by an old established actor—Spencer

Tracy. However, he dies early in the film but appears throughout as a kind of guardian angel to Johnson, who has been his favorite among the men. He now accompanies the younger man everywhere, both in the air and when he is off duty. But, of course, only the cinema audience can see him. This presents certain problems when romance enters the story. As it happens, the young pilot begins to woo his former commander's woman. She is also a pilot and ferries aircraft between airfields.

After a number of exciting air battles, everything turns out for the best when the heroine is reunited with her man (Tracy) in the flyers' heaven and the audience could leave the cinema knowing that they had seen a decent film about flying, but nothing more.

The second female lead was played by Esther Williams, who for a change did not appear as a beautiful swimmer—or did she? It is so easy to forget after so many years; could she have been involved in some little *tête-à-tête* on a beach?

The other film, *PILOT 5,* had Franchot Tone, Gene Kelly, Marsha Hunt and, once again, Van Johnson in the cast. It concerns a small group of pilots who are left behind on a tiny field in the jungles of the Philippines. The Americans have retreated from the area and it is now occupied by the Japanese.

From left: Van Johnson, Barry Nelson, Don DeFore and Spencer Tracy in A GUY NAMED JOE (1943).

Because communications have broken down, the squadron is unaware of what has happened. The whole time they await orders. The squadron is equipped with the relatively obsolete fighter Republic Seversky EP-1, and they are also low on fuel. Despite this fact, they engage the very fast and highly maneuverable Zero in battle with ruinous consequences. One pilot after another is shot down.

The story has a kind of tired monotony about it, but the director George Sidney does manage to capture the hopeless atmosphere

Franchot Tone has crash-landed his Seversky EP-1 in PILOT 5 (1943).

Facing page: Dana Andrews (left) and Don Ameche in WING AND A PRAYER (1944).

LIFE JACKET DYE
TO RELEASE DYE PULL TAB

Dane Clark in GOD IS MY CO-PILOT (1945).

of isolation while the men await orders that never come.

We would like to mention, as a curiosity, that the type of aircraft used in the film was originally intended to be shipped to Sweden, which at the time almost completely lacked modern airplanes. Only a few of these aircraft were actually delivered to the Swedish Air Force. The remainder were confiscated and sent to the Philippines instead as reinforcements!

A WING AND A PRAYER was based upon the battle of Midway in 1942. The film was released in 1944. Produced by Fox and directed by Henry Hathaway, it starred Don Ameche, Dana Andrews, Kevin O'Shea, Charles Bickford and Sir Cedric Hardwicke. Some originality was shown in the fact that not a single woman appears in the film, if we disregard the pinups attached to locker doors.

Don Ameche played the tough, ruthless officer who commanded his troops with a penetrating eye. But, of course, in his heart he was the one who sweated and suffered the most everytime his pilots flew a mission.

The action took place entirely on board an aircraft carrier and in the air above Midway. It displayed much authentic air-battle footage, frequently taken with wing-mounted cameras. The description of life on board the carrier was realistic and interesting, and comprised indeed the whole action of the film. It was not, alas, a film of any great depth.

The cinema audience were able to get their fill of authenticity and realism in two great documentaries produced in 1944. One, *MEMPHIS BELLE,* has already been mentioned. But William Wyler also made a film for the U.S. Navy and Fox, a kind of filmic hymn in praise of the American Navy and all its men. It was called *THE FIGHTING LADY* and concerned a real aircraft carrier—a floating city with its own airfield. The film showed the men on board—the seamen who ensure that these gigantic juggernauts functioned, and the flyers who were sent out on missions of extreme danger and whose return to the ship often took place in total darkness. For many, there was no return at all.

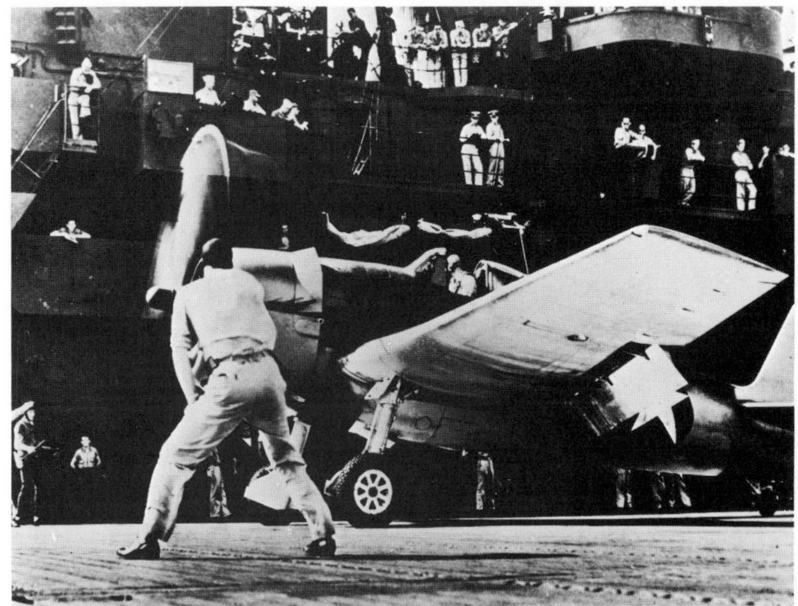

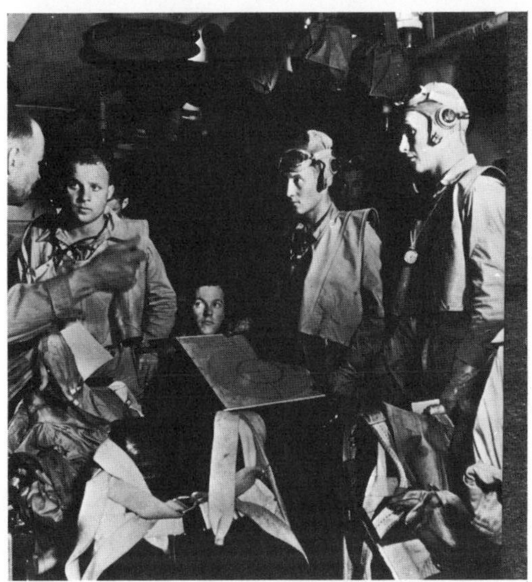

Some stills from the unforgettable THE FIGHTING LADY (1944), *a film which through its very high technical and human qualities takes a place high on the best list. Top: A Grumman F6F Hellcat takes off; to the left some pilots get their orders before the mission starts. Below: A Japanese torpedo bomber—a Nakajima B5N5 Kate—has just been set on fire.*

Van Johnson and Robert Walker in Metro's air adventure of 1944—THIRTY SECONDS OVER TOKYO.

Spencer Tracy as Colonel James Doolittle in THIRTY SECONDS OVER TOKYO (1944).

The audience could feel what it was like to approach an object that at first sighting looked much like a tombstone bobbing on the angry surface of the sea. How it was to attempt to land on the flight deck, perhaps in the middle of the night in an aircraft so badly damaged that it flew more out of habit than by the skill of the pilot, its wings and its engine. Crash landings were many and in some cases almost unbelievable.

How is it that so much of the "real thing" could be preserved? The fact is that both the U.S. Navy and the Marines themselves filmed all starts and landings on all their aircraft carriers, and still do. In addition to this, all the "machine gun" film taken by the wing cameras on the aircraft was also kept. A whole staff of technicians and photographers were retained to take further shots and edit the material; it was headed by the famous photographer Edward J. Steichen.

In 1944 it became fashionable to make feature films about the war as realistic and authentic as possible. If they were not all completely documentary, they were close to it—films based on real events and experience. One such film was *THIRTY SECONDS OVER TOKYO,* made by Metro-Goldwyn-Mayer under the austere direction of Mervyn LeRoy.

This was based on a book of the same name written by Ted E. Lawson, a young American flyer. Lawson was one of a number of crew members especially chosen by the then Colonel James Doolittle. The purpose was to train them for surprise raids on Tokyo. This was 1942 and Uncle Sam was still licking his wounds and had not yet struck back for the ignominious attack in December of the previous year. But plans to do so were being laid. During the time these were being prepared, it was considered important to give the Japanese a bloody nose. This was achieved with the raid that was so excellently portrayed in Lawson's book and the Metro film.

The film follows the men from the time the crews are chosen through their training and up to their dramatic start from the aircraft carrier *Hornet.* The type of aircraft used—B-25 Mitchells—had never before taken off from the deck of a carrier and many considered it a risky venture. But the only way to get sufficiently close to the Japanese islands was to transport the planes by sea. However, the flotilla of ships was discovered and the bombers were forced to take off a day earlier than planned. There was a full storm blowing and it looked as though they would fail. Nevertheless, Doolittle ordered his planes up despite the danger—as a matter of fact, his own aircraft was the first to take off. The actual start was wholly successful and all the aircraft began the mission. They approached their target flying very low and dumped their bombs on the Japanese capital.

Unfortunately, during their continued flight to safe bases in China, a number of planes were forced down or crashed. The crews of some of these were captured by the Japanese and shortly thereafter were executed, following a highly questionable trial.

Lawson's own plane, called *The Ruptured Duck,* crash-landed near the Chinese coast. It was a violent crash and Lawson was severely injured. But the crew was well taken care of by the local Chinese population and then guided to the safety of an American air base. This phase of the operation was very well told and highly exciting in its realism.

Lawson and his crew return to America and he is reunited with his wife. He has, however, suffered a personal tragedy in that one of his legs had to be amputated during the long agonizing escape.

Authentic film material was used from the time of takeoff, the approach to target and the final bombing of Tokyo—the actual bombing lasted only thirty seconds. Lawson was played sympathetically by Van Johnson and Lawson's wife by Phyllis Thaxter, who made her debut in this film.

The role of Jimmy Doolittle was portrayed by Spencer Tracy, that marvelous actor who never "blew" a role.

THE PURPLE HEART, a film about the fate of the crewmen taken prisoners by the Japanese forces, also was made in 1944. Among the many good players in the cast was Dana Andrews, who appeared as a crew captain.

Because the film was based on a true story, it had a strong dramatic impact for audiences of Americans who knew that the Japanese had killed most of the captive airmen.

Film footage of the actual mission was used in the 1944 film. That same footage can be seen today in Cinerama in the title sequence for *THE BATTLE OF THE MIDWAY* (1976).

An even more realistic film was made about the Flying Tigers and their operations on behalf of Chiang Kai-shek. Based on Robert Lee Scott's autobiographical book of the same title, Warner Brothers made *GOD IS MY CO-PILOT* in 1945.

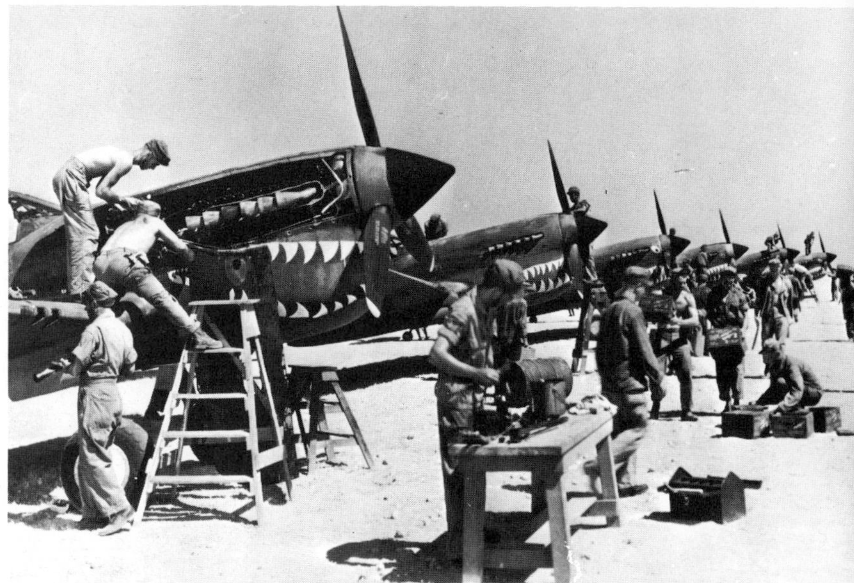

The Curtiss P-40s get their service between missions. From GOD IS MY CO-PILOT (1945).

Raymond Massey as General Claire Chennault in GOD IS MY CO-PILOT (1945).

Colonel Jeff Nixon (Robert Walker) had one of the key roles in Metro's nuclear drama THE BEGINNING OR THE END (1948).

Scott was a former colonel in the U.S. Army Air Force who had been told that he was too old at age 34 to fly fighter planes anymore. He then left the air force and signed on with Claire Chennault's American Voluntary Group (AVG) to serve in China. (See *FLYING TIGERS,* page 72.)

Flying Curtiss P-40s, the Tigers fought the Japanese Air Force during late 1941 before the attack on Pearl Harbor.

Chennault had placed Scott in command of the flying squadrons. The book describes his exciting times from his first takeoff until the day he turned his command over to the regular American forces in 1942.

Robert Florey directed this project and made a good air movie. Dennis Morgan had the role of the "over-the-hill" colonel. Raymond Massey played General Chennault, and Alan Hale took the role of a clergyman. Dane Clark appeared as one of Scott's pilots.

Many of the Flying Tiger pilots became fighter aces. Some of them went on to make their careers in the Air Force and Navy. Those who did so and also survived the war years were Scott, Colonel David "Tex" Hill, Major Albert "Ajax" Baumler and Gregory "Pappy" Boyington.

By 1945, however, it was all over. The terminal point was something called "the Big Bomb." Metro told the story of this terrifying, dangerous weapon in the 1948 film *THE BEGINNING OR THE END.*

We all know today that Professor Robert Oppenheimer had been working on "Project Manhattan" in utmost secrecy. He carried out this work with a number of selected scientists of various nationalities. Together they worked on this project for many years and then on June 6, 1945, they detonated the first atomic bomb. Far out in the desert of New Mexico, they witnessed an event that few people believed possible. We will never know what they thought and felt at the very moment the huge mushroom cloud expanded above them and the earth shook under them. We know that the effect of the bomb was terrible indeed and that despite this President Truman gave the order to drop it on selected targets in Japan.

THE BEGINNING OR THE END was an honest, if somewhat romantic, description of how this incredible instrument of destruction was built. It told of the technical and human problems involved. Norman Taurog directed it for Metro-Goldwyn-Mayer and it is generally acknowledged that he did so successfully. The cast included such names as Brian Donlevy, Robert Walker, Tom Drake and Audrey Totter.

Unfortunately this disturbing document is largely forgotten in film circles. But the fact is that it was the first public presentation of "what actually happened over there." There was original footage from the actual dropping of the first bomb over Hiroshima. Some of the shots, paradoxically, were so beautifully filmed as to be almost nauseating in retrospect.

Thus a time of terror in the brief history of mankind ended and the dark clouds lifted from our planet to make way for a new era—a time of light . . . or? . . .

Dennis Morgan played Colonel Robert Lee Scott in Warner Bros.' GOD IS MY CO-PILOT

In Other Skies

It is worth noting that in addition to the British, American, German and Japanese films that we have named in the preceding chapters, there were also a number of films about flying made in other countries, primarily in Europe.

Spain succeeded in remaining neutral during the Second World War, but between 1936 and 1939 the country went through a crushing civil war. It came to an end in 1939 when the Republican side was forced to surrender to the rebel nationalist forces of General Francisco Franco.

The Fascists received considerable help from Germany and Italy, help which included some aircraft. Germany also assisted the nationalists with a "volunteer" air force—actually a means of testing Germany's air strength before the coming world conflict. The infamous Condor Legion was really nothing more nor less than a detachment of the Luftwaffe which, equipped with Heinkel He 111s and Dornier Do 17 bombers and the most modern fighter planes, were given their final "polish" in the air battles above the Spanish earth—"polish" which included the notorious raid over Guernica.

Many films have been made about this war—a grim dress rehearsal for the greater horrors to come—but few of them had to do with flying. In 1941, however, the Spanish themselves made *ESCUADRILLA (Squadron),* directed by Antonio Román. Some of Spain's most well-known stars appeared in it: Alfredo Mayo, Luchy Soto and José Nieto.

The Swedish actor Stig Järrel as Lieutenant Sperling in the dive-bomber drama FÖRSTA DIVISIONEN (1941) (The First Squadron).

The film was about fighter pilots on the nationalist side. Two of them are in love with the same girl (a not uncommon theme . . . right?). She lives on an estate in the province of Cordova, where the squadron is based. Since she has been educated abroad she has difficulty understanding the political situation at home in Spain. A number of complications arise in connection with both these subjects.

Among Spanish flyers, too, there was a fantastic comradeship. For some of them, comradeship in death. One of the two rivals for the girl gets into difficulties in an air battle, but his friend heroically sacrifices his life to save him. The object of their love and rivalry suddenly realizes what the war is all about and zealously joins the cause of freedom!

Unfortunately, it is all rather thin, but there is some drama in the unusually well-filmed and realistic flying sequences. There are also a number of authentic air-battle scenes in a film that is otherwise all heroics and propaganda.

On the Republican side, there were volunteers from many nations. The International Brigade also fought to free Spain and received material help from a number of nations including the Soviet Union. This latter country sent a large number of fighter planes, but they were mostly obsolete and were no match for nationalist fighters, which were Italian Fiat Cr 32s, German Heinkel He 51s and Messerschmitt Me 109s. The small Russian I-15 Chatka and the I-16 Rata were maneuverable but not fast enough to maintain air superiority.

I have not been able to find any Spanish films about flying on the Republican side, but in France André Malraux made the historical *L'ESPOIR* (1938) with a considerable amount of authentic material—even flying sequences—from the Civil War. A relatively modern story made in 1957 tells about a pilot officer who fought the war on the nationalist side. His special task was to infiltrate behind enemy lines. The film was called *HEROES DEL AIR (Heroes of the Air)* and it also had Alfredo Mayo in the leading role—as the middle-aged Colonel Rivas.

The story is as follows: at a base in Barajas, there is much excitement awaiting the arrival of an aircraft belonging to the Air Rescue Service. It is in the middle of the fifties. The plane is flown by Captain Alfredo Soler (Julio Núnez). He crashes the plane on landing but escapes with his life. Rivas, commander of the Air Rescue Service, orders an investigation into the crash.

He recalls in flashbacks how he first met Soler. It was during the Civil War in 1938. At the time, Rivas was leader of a fighter squadron and he meets Soler among a number of new pilot recruits who have just come to the squadron. The young pilot had made a deep impression on Rivas by his bravery, his competence, and his willingness to volunteer for the most dangerous missions.

Rivas himself has been ordered to try to infiltrate the "Red" side. He succeeds in this and flies for a time as a "loyal Republican" in a government squadron (compare with *SQUADRON LEADER X,* 1943). When he has gained the information he sought, he heads back to his own lines in a stolen plane. Lieutenant Soler just happens to be out on a patrol flight at the same time (have we heard this before?). He spots the enemy aircraft and attacks it—he does not know, of course, that Rivas is the pilot. A wild air battle ensues and in the end Rivas is shot down by his young antagonist. He is badly injured but survives. When he is being treated in the

From the Spanish film ESCUADRILLA (1941). *Alfredo Mayo (right) has something to say to his colleague, José Niéto.*

Fascist fighters attack in the Italian L'ARMATA AZZURRA (1935) (The Winged Armada).

hospital, he meets Isabel (Lina Rosales). She is a beautiful young widow and also the sister of Soler. They fall in love and get married.

After the war is over Rivas becomes head of the Air Rescue Service and employs his brother-in-law. Now suddenly Isabel's former husband reappears—he was not dead after all—and demands money from his wife to keep his mouth shut and disappear. They come to an agreement and Isabel's brother promises to help her. He will fly the money to a small concealed airfield, and he does this in one of the Rescue Service's aircraft that he has "borrowed." The villain in the story is not satisfied with just the money but demands to be flown to safety over the border. Soler refuses and the two men fight until finally the blackmailing husband is killed by one of the plane's propellors. Soler is injured but flies his plane back to base and the circle is completed, for it is precisely this crash landing that opened the film. The crash is caused because his injuries from the fight make it impossible for him to land the plane safely. Isabel tells her husband all and the film ends as Rivas realizes that his brother-in-law is both a great pilot and good friend.

Now we come to an Italian film from 1934. Some claim it was made in 1932 and others 1935. The exact year *L'ARMATA AZZURRA (The Winged Armada)* was premiered is of little importance; it is of greater interest to note that it was directed by Gennaro Righelli and that it was a work of pure propaganda, the intention of which was to glorify the powerful Italian air fleet. This power was displayed by having veritable armadas of aircraft pass across the silver screen from all directions. The aerial photography was quite fantastic.

The first Swedish film to focus on flying was *LUFTENS VAGABOND* (Vagabond of the Air). Produced by Europa Film in 1933 and directed by the versatile Weyler Hildebrand, the movie has a melodramatic plot, but beautiful flying sequences.

Hiker Gull Werner (Aino Taube) is injured. A flying ambulance is summoned and lands on a nearby lake. The two pilots are Gustav Falk (Albin Ahrenberg) and Gunnar Onell (Ake Ohberg). Falk recognizes the in-

From left: Henrik Dyfverman, Arnold Sjöstrand, Willy Peters and Oscar Törnblom as young air cadets in the Swedish UNGDOM AV IDAG (1936) (Youth of Today).

The Swedish UNGDOM AV IDAG (1936) (Youth of Today).

jured girl as an old love. But this time he has competition from his fellow pilot. Gunnar gets the girl; Falk goes off on a polar expedition and dies in a crash.

The actor who played Falk, Albin Ahrenberg (1889–1968), was in real life one of Sweden's best-known pilots. He tried to initiate regular flights to the United States in 1929, but the first trip was aborted in Greenland because of bad weather, and the project was dropped. For many years, Ahrenberg piloted his Junker aircraft on tours around Sweden to promote flying. (The author flew for the first time, at the age of five, on an Ahrenberg flight.)

Some of the best flying sequences in the film show the ambulance making its way over the dark northern forests and through the polar night with only the light from ground fires as landmarks.

The well-known theater director Per-Axel Branner attempted a real blue/gold flying story. It was made in 1936 and the title was *UNGDOM AV IDAG (Youth of Today)* and the location was the flying-training school of the Swedish Air Force. In the film, the audience could follow the progress of the young pilots on their way to earn their golden wings. The critics maintained that it was a charming portrayal of young men being shaped into pilots, and included in the cast were such names as Carl Barcklind, Kotti Chave, Arnold Sjöstrand, Anne-Marie Brunius and Gösta Cederlund.

From 1936 up to the present, there have not been many Swedish films on the subject of flying. Those that have been produced have almost exclusively dealt with the daily routine of military flying. *FÖRSTA DIVISIONEN (The First Squadron),* made by Terra Film in 1941, was no exception. During the war years when Hitler rattled his sword beyond this country's borders and put the jackboot down in Denmark and Norway, the Swedish Air Force, which was in a state of busy rearmament, tried to show that it was well prepared in the case of attack.

There was excellent cooperation between the Air Force and Terra Film and the young director Hasse Ekman was able to make a remarkably good flying film for its time that

The Swedish FÖRSTA DIVISIONEN (1941) (The First Squadron).

showed the everyday life of a dive-bomber squadron.

FÖRSTA DIVISIONEN had a fine dramatic line blended with overtones of light humor—and something of this kind was doubtless what the public wished to see during that difficult time. Lars Hanson, one of the great names in Swedish film, played Wing Commander Stålberg and some of his young pilots were played by Stig Järrel, Gunnar Sjöberg, Kotti Chave and Hasse Ekman himself.

A brief resumé: young Flying Officer Bråde (Ekman) is just returning to his unit after having spent some time in a hospital following a crash. He is to serve in the 1st Squadron. In the same squadron there is also the untrustworthy Billman (Chave) and Rutger Sperling (Järrel), a monocled man capable of flying like the devil himself if it suits him to do so.

During a bombing test, Bråde gets a bomb in his propellor and is forced to abandon his plane. He parachutes down right into the target area. The Wing Commander who had been following the operation from his own plane realizes that Bråde's situation is critical

Colonel Ståhlberg (Lars Hanson) saves his injured young pilot Bråde (Hasse Ekman), after he has parachuted from his dive-bomber right into the target area. From the Swedish film FÖRSTA DIVISIONEN (1941).

and succeeds in landing his aircraft in a small adjacent field. He makes his way to the young pilot whose leg is injured. He succeeds in helping him out of range of the bombs his comrades are unwittingly dropping all around them.

After a time, Sperling learns that he is going blind. He is forced to give up flying: a fate worse than death for someone who loves the freedom of the air. His comrades give him a farewell dinner party in the mess. Stålberg looks on as his unfortunate young pilot abruptly gets up and leaves the festivities. He feels that something is wrong and goes discreetly out after him. He discovers the young man holding his service revolver in his hand. They exchange only a few words and then return to the others who are loudly enjoying themselves in the mess.

After having been operated on, Sperling comes back one day to his old unit to visit his friends. He looks healthy—at least he gives the impression of health—but in actual fact he can barely see.

While talking to his old Squadron Leader (Sjöberg), the latter, in a weak moment, agrees to let the ex-flyer go along as signaler in the aft cockpit of a plane out on a night flight. Sperling is as happy as a child as he checks out the equipment for the flight. He is to fly with Bråde whose regular signaler is on leave.

The flight takes off and everything appears to be normal. But then fog is reported at the air base and the fields in the vicinity. All the pilots are called home and they land at the last minute as thick fog closes in. All except Bråde and Sperling. Their radio broke down at the beginning of the flight and they never heard the order to return to base. When they do return the airfield is completely closed in by fog and without their radio they cannot make an instrument landing. Bråde orders Sperling to jump but he refuses: "I'm comfortable where I am, now that I'm back in the seat of a plane again."

Although all odds are against him, Bråde attempts a landing. It is doomed to failure and ends, as expected, in disaster. They crash and are both killed.

The Swedish actor George Fant in the test pilot epic TRE SÖNER GICK TILL FLYGET (1945) (Three Sons Joined the Air Force).

Seeing this film today, as a professional flyer, I cannot help smiling a little. So much of it is no longer true and it is so easy to forget what flying was like in those days. But if we consider when it was made, then it holds up very well. Järrel's portrayal of Sperling was excellent and it represented a dramatic breakthrough for him in Swedish movies. In the years to come he became one of the big names in the Swedish film world.

Up until 1945 nothing new in the way of films about flying occurred in Sweden, but in that year there appeared a movie about a test pilot attached to an aircraft factory (SAAB). The film was titled *TRE SÖNER GICK TILL FLYGET (Three Sons Joined the Air Force)* and appearing as the three Hallman brothers—all of whom became pilots—were George Fant, Göran Gentele and Stig Olin. It was beautifully filmed and gave an accurate picture of the standard of the Swedish Air Force and aircraft industry. Two completely Swedish-made aircraft were used in the film, the B-17 and B-18A, both from the drawing boards of SAAB and both good examples of Swedish engineering.

Next page, top: Sven Lindberg is saved from his burning Flying Barrel. From the Swedish GULA DIVISIONEN (1954) (The Yellow Squadron).

Next page, left: Stig Olin and Bengt Ekroth have a serious talk in TRE SÖNER GICK TILL FLYGET (1945).

Far right: Hasse Ekman as the Squadron Leader in GULA DIVISIONEN (1954).

In 1949, there was a Swedish/Norwegian coproduction called *VI FLYGER PÅ RIO (We Head for Rio)* which tried to show the hardships of Swedish and Norwegian pilots on the newly established flying routes to South America. They flew DC-4s and Åke Ohberg, Lars Nordrum, Margareta Fahlén, Lauritz Falk and Per Oscarsson unraveled various intrigues into which had been woven a fair portion of romance. The film was directed by Ohberg and although it was no masterpiece it provided a pleasant and relatively convincing picture of the daily life of airline pilots. There was an authentic crash scene in the film that was first shown in *UNGDOM AV IDAG (Youth of Today)*.

In 1954, Stig Olin made a film called *GULA DIVISIONEN (The Yellow Squadron)* about one of the most famous of all Swedish aircraft, the SAAB J-29, "The Flying Barrel." The leading roles were taken by Hasse Ekman, Sven Lindberg, Lars Ekborg and

The navigator (Olle Johansson) tries desperately to keep the pilot (Runar Martholm) alive. From the Swedish FLYGPLAN SAKNAS (1965) (Missing Aircraft).

A scene from the French L'EQUIPAGE (1935) (The Crew). *To the left, the pilot and husband (Charles Vanel) and behind, in the rear cockpit, the young observer and lover (Jean-Pierre Aumont) of the pilot's wife (Annabella).*

Gertrud Fridh. The purpose of the film, perhaps, was to try to repeat the success of *FÖRSTA DIVISIONEN* in 1941. Unfortunately, it failed in this, despite all the excellent flying scenes. The screenplay was based on a novel by Lars Widding entitled *Gyllene Vingar (Golden Wings)* but most of the quality of the book was lost so that the film was too bland.

An advanced gimmick was used in a sequence when the film's "bad boy" flies a training plane with his girlfriend along as passenger. To show off to her, he flies under one of Stockholm's bridges and ends by doing a loop over and under the bridge.

There were no new vapor trails seen on Swedish movie screens until 1965 when Per Gunwall attempted to make a modern tale about flying. Its title was *FLYGPLAN SAKNAS (Missing Aircraft)* and was about a reconnaissance plane, S-32 Lansen, and its crew of two. During a long flight over the sea, the engine stops and they are forced to leave the aircraft in catapult seats. The pilot (Runar Martholm) and his navigator (Olle Johansson) land in the sea but manage to climb into their rubber dinghies. The pilot is severely injured after the jump—broken leg, internal injuries and shock. Fortunately, they land fairly close to each other and the navigator manages to paddle his dinghy over to the pilot's and fasten them both together. Then they await their rescue, which they believe will be soon. But it is long in coming. It takes some time to organize the search, and we follow it from the moment they are reported missing until they are picked up—the pilot is now dead—and taken on board a destroyer. The drama of the two men lost at sea is shown in a series of brief cuts as the rescue operations progress.

It was a good idea but not very well executed. However, in the beginning of the film there are some remarkable flying scenes and the drama between the two men has a touch of realism. Since then silence has reigned in the Swedish film industry as regards films about flying.

In the comments on Spanish and Italian flying films it was indicated that there were a number of blank spaces in the author's knowledge of this genre. For example, the Soviet Union has not been thoroughly researched due to the difficulties involved in obtaining facts and finding sources; the same is true of Eastern Europe generally. Despite the difficulties, however, I have succeeded in obtaining some information on Russian, Czechoslovakian, Polish and East German films in which the action has to do with flying.

But before we move eastward, let us have a look at France. This great film land should be able to show a rich harvest if one searched the archives and encyclopedias thoroughly. Certainly the French have made a fair number of films about flying and flyers, but it has proved astonishingly difficult to obtain source material. But one famous flying story—virtually a classic—can be described here.

In 1924 Joseph Kessel wrote a novel called *L'Equipage,* which provided the basis for a film of the same name made in 1928. It was a silent film, but a new version with sound was made in 1935 by one of central Europe's greatest directors, Anatole Litvak. It is about a French youth who goes to the front in the First World War. His duty is to serve as lookout in an aircraft flown by a heartily disliked middle-aged lieutenant. Jean-Pierre Aumont played the gentle young man and Charles Vanel the brusque, sullen pilot.

After a time, the young man discovers that the woman he has fallen deeply in love with is the wife of the man who sits in the cockpit in front of him. As good a triangle drama as one could imagine! The wife (Annabella) responds to the young man's feelings and they begin an affair. The husband knows all about it but does not let on. During a flight he is severely wounded but succeeds in flying his aircraft back to base. However, the young man sitting in the aft cockpit is dead. The husband is taken to hospital where he is looked after by his wife. They fall in love again and everything turns out happily, but he never reveals that he knew about her young lover all along.

Certain parts of the film have elements of high drama. The front line has exactly the gray realism and hopelessness that one would imagine, and the drama between the two

Director Jean Renoir is at left in this photo from the cynical French drama LA REGLE DU JEU (1936) (The Rules of the Game).

men is intensely felt. And the flying scenes must be given a pass mark for realism.

Oddly enough, when Litvak went to the United States a few years later, the first film he made was an American version of the same story. This time it was given the title *THE WOMAN I LOVE* (1937) and starred Louis Hayward, Paul Muni and Miriam Hopkins in the roles of the young lover, the husband and his wife, respectively. Many of the locations and flying scenes from the earlier French version were also used in this film—which, however, never quite achieved the same atmosphere as its predecessor.

Jean Renoir included a flying sequence in his 1939 film *LA REGLE DU JEU* (The Rules of the Game). It is actually an examination of the manners and morals of Europe in that era. However, one of the leading characters is a pilot, Andre Jurieu (Roland Toutain). Jurieu has performed a Lindbergh-like achievement in flying across the Atlantic, but his conduct on landing is not heroic. He angers the press and the worshipping public by being more interested in his mistress than glory. Later, he is accidentally shot by a forest ranger and dies meaninglessly—having survived the dangerous flight and attendant publicity.

Renoir's message is that there are no uplifting rules in the game of life and death, nor methods of survival. "To die in the pilot seat of a winged machine is the same damned way of dying as sitting in a rocking chair in the middle of a burning building."

NORMANDIA-NIEMAN (1960) is a Soviet-French production. Jean Dreville directed the film about a French fighter squadron attached to Russian forces during the Second World War. The squadron flew Soviet-built Yak 3 and Yak 9 aircraft. These were relatively effective in air battles with the Germans on the Eastern Front.

Red Wings

Let us end this chapter with a closer look at flying dramas coming from Eastern skies.

The flying films from the Soviet Union could be said to have developed in direct conjunction with the progress of technical achievements in that vast but isolated land. The political tension between the Soviet and the West has also certainly influenced the content of its films.

In accordance with Stalin's theories ("the growth of the class struggle with the progress of socialism"), many of the films from the Soviet Union have been populated with spies and "enemies of the people." Such a film is *AEROGRAD (Air City)** from 1935, made by the Ukrainian director Aleksandr Dovzhenko. The action of the film was set in the Far East and told of erstwhile big farmers, sectarians and Japanese spies. Dovzhenko ended the film with a parade of 1,000 aircraft flying building materials to a new pioneer city.

However, it was not all politics even though a considerable amount of propaganda was slipped in in one way or another. In some films one could follow the training of Soviet military pilots. One example is *LIOTTJIKI (The Aviators)* from 1935, directed by Julij Rajzman, and another is *KRYLATYJ MALJAR (The Flying Painter).*

One film about Russian civil aviation *VOZDUSJNAJA POTJATA (Air Mail)* (1939), tells about a female pilot and her hardships when she atttempts to fly medicines to an isolated children's hospital in the Far East.

Nor is the amorous triangle, so well known in English-language films, missing from Russian movies. This rather more private motif could be enjoyed in *ISTREBITELI (Fighter Planes)* from 1939.

As the tensions increased along the country's frontiers so too did the number of films of a more "patriotic" character (of the *Air City* type). One of these was Mikhail Kalatozov's *MUZJESTVO (Bravery),* released in

*All Russian film titles are literal translations from the original Russian.

The young Russian pilot Valerij Chjkalov is lifted aloft by his comrades in celebration of a successful mission from VALERIJ CHJKALOV (1940).

NEBESNYJ TICHOCHOD (1945) (Sky Flight).

1940. Briefly, it is about a heroic Russian pilot who contributes to the capture of a foreign spy. The strength of the film lies in its flying sequences. The hero, the pilot Tomilin (played by Oleg Chjakov), is a bit of a boaster, but eventually he gains the admiration of everyone during a dramatic struggle inside an airplane when by brilliant maneuvers of the aircraft he manages to thwart the spy's efforts to hijack the plane.

Not long before Hitler began his attack on the Soviet Union there was a film about a very well known Russian pilot whose name provided its title—*VALERIJ CHJKALOV*. It was a story about his life and achievements and his development from a young, irresponsible practical joker into a dutifully zealous flyer— all in the pattern of social realism.

There were ten or so films made in the Soviet Union about the air battle on the Eastern Front, among which were everything from serious dramas to slightly comic efforts with a fair portion of sentimentality. Among the films produced in 1941 was *ESKADRILJA NR. 5 (The 5th Squadron),* directed by Avram Room. And if this could be seen as a serious film then *KRYLATYJ TZVOSTJIK (An Air Taxi)* from 1943 was a considerably lighter effort. It was about a love affair between Natasha (Ludmila Chelikovskaja) and the daring pilot Baranov (Michail Zjarov) and his heroic deeds in the air battles against the Germans.

POVEST O NASTOJASJTJEM TJELOVEKE (1948) (The Story of a Real Man).

The same couple of actors also appeared in *BESPOKOJNOJE CHOZJAJSTVO (Falsely Equipped)* (1946). They were in charge of a phony air base where all the buildings and aircraft were really only dummies, a decoy to induce German pilots to drop their bombs on totally worthless targets.

Another rather light film was *NEBESNYJ TICHOCHOD (The Sky Flight)* from 1945, which told the story of the daily life of the pilots belonging to a light aircraft reconnaissance squadron; the tale was told with large portions of humor and accompanied by popular music.

Other films about the war were *DOROGA K ZVIOZDAM (The Way to the Stars)* from 1942 and *ZDI MENJA (Wait for Me)* (1943). *NEBO MOSKVY (The Moscow Sky)* was released in 1944 and *NASJE SERDTSE (Our Heart)* in 1946. The latter is a memorable film about a Soviet aeronautical engineer and his efforts during the war to improve on the construction of Russian aircraft, to make them more efficient weapons and increase their speed. Their development of a jet aircraft at that time was not in agreement with the facts. However, in the film it was of course a success and the movie ends with a grandiose nonstop flight around the world.

One of the best known postwar films about flying was called *POVEST O NASTOJASJTJEM TJELOVEKE (The Story of a Real Man).* It was similar to a couple of films made in the West, although they were done somewhat later, about a flyer who has lost both his legs. Despite this handicap, he learns to walk again and even how to dance, but most important of all he is able to fly again. Alexsej Meressiev was such a pilot and in the film he was portrayed with a psychological warmth and authenticity by Pavel Kadotjnikov.

After the war the number of films produced was sharply reduced generally and there were very few flying films made during Stalin's last years. However, in 1950 there was a film biography of one of Russia's great pioneers in the field of aerodynamics and aircraft construction. It was entitled *ZUKOVSKI* and was directed by Vsevolod Pudovkin.

During the latter part of the fifties, a few more flying films were made. Most of them concerned the war years, such as *BAL-*

TIJSKOJE NEBO (Baltic Sky) (1961) and *NORMANDIA-NIEMAN.*

The problem of civilian flying and the training of pilots was adequately dealt with in *ZVEZDY NA KRYLJACK (Winged Stars)* made in 1950.

There is not a single flying film to be found among the propaganda films dealing with "the Cold War." There is, however, a Czechoslovakian film of this type called *UNOS (Hijacking).* It was made in 1952 and concerned the skyjacking of a plane to West Germany. One of the historical ironies associated with this film is that one of its two directors, Jan Kadar, has lived in exile in the United States since 1968—the country most severely criticized in the film.

One of the most powerful films attacking the criminal actions of Stalinism was called *TJISTOJE NEBO (Clear Sky).* This film was directed by Grigorij Tjuchrai and concerns a famous test pilot, Alexsej Astachov (played by Jevgeni Urbanski), who was believed to have crashed in an air battle and has been declared dead. In actual fact, he is taken prisoner by the Germans. When he returns home after the war he is accused, like so many others, of being a traitor. He is expelled from the Party and not allowed to fly again. After this relatively mild reprisal (if one compares it to the real penalties given for such "crimes"), he is eventually completely rehabilitated and in the final heavily symbolic sequence we see him once again piloting a Soviet plane up into the clear blue heavens.

During the sixties, space films began to appear in the East too. Most of them were made shortly after the flight of the first "Sputnik" in 1957 and following Yuri Gagarin's journey into space in 1959. There are more than ten films from the period either about the Soviet "father" of the space age, Constantine Tsiolkovski, or more or less straightforward science-fiction dramas. One film about Tsiolkovski was made in 1958. It was

IM POKORIJAJETSIA NJEBO (1963) (Masters of the Sky). *In the foreground is glimpsed a Ilushin Il-2 Shturmovik. Sleek fighter plane is a Lavochkin La-7.*

called *TJELOVEK Z PLANETY ZEMLJA (The Man from the Planet Earth).*

The newest and most expensive science-fiction effort is Andrei Tarkovski's *SOLARIS.* It was based on a novel by the Polish science-fiction writer Stanislaw Lem. It may be regarded as an East European counterpart at an opposite philosophical pole to Stanley Kubrick's *2001—A SPACE ODYSSEY* made in 1968.

Among the remaining flying films from the sixties, I would like to mention *V METRVOJ PETLE (Death Loop)* (1963) about some of the pioneers of Russian aviation, with the emphasis on Serge Utotikin. The same year there was a new version of the construction of the first Soviet jet plane, *IM POKORIJAJETSIA NEBO (Masters of the Sky).* This film, incidentally, received first prize at a festival for flying films in France in 1963.

There was an interesting film made by the female Russian director Larisa Sjepitkos in 1966 called *KRYLJA (Wings).* It dealt with the flying profession on a psychological level. The heroine of the film—ex-flying ace Nadiezda Pietruchina—is shown in a conflict-filled situation: for health reasons she is no longer able to practice her profession. But in the final scenes we see Pietruchina smiling happily again as she sits at the controls of an airplane. . . .

In 1967 there were two films about the Second World War. *MESTA TUT TICHIJE (Calm Places)* dealt with the battle against German U-boats in the Barents Sea and *CHRONIKA PIKURUJUSJTJEGO BOMBARDIROVSJTJIKA (The Story of a Dive Bomber)* told about three young flyers fighting for their country in a dive-bomber squadron. Before the film ends all three have given their lives in the heroic struggle for the cause.

The Soviet Union has also produced a number of feature-length, or longer, documentary films about flying. One of these *KRYLIA OKTIABRIA (October Wings)* was released in 1967. It was simply a film report of a vast aviation display held just outside Moscow in 1966. Another documentary, entitled *LJUDI ZEMLI I NEBA (People of the Earth and Sky),* was released in 1969. It was the filmed biography of a pilot by the name of Serge Garnajev.

The most recent Soviet film on flying was released in 1979. *EKIPAZJ* (The Crew) was directed by Alexander Mitta. This is a rather weak imitation of the American *AIRPORT* film series, with some Russian additions to the cliches of catastrophe. The flying sequences are of reasonably good quality.

The lives of various crew members of an Aeroflot passenger plane—a Tupolev Tu 154—are interwoven as the plot leads up to the climax. The high point of the film is the rescue of a large number of people from an area threatened by a volcano. The plane finally makes it off the ground, but once in the air, an engine fails and the aircraft loses altitude rapidly. Disaster appears inevitable, but the heroes succeed in the miraculous trick of repairing the faulty engine by getting out on the engine gondolas (in the aft section of the plane) while the craft plunges at great speed through the frigid atmosphere. It all ends happily, and they land safely at Moscow.

Whereas the Soviet Russian cinema has produced a fairly large number of flying films—approximately fifty features since 1935—this particular subject is more modestly represented in the other countries of Eastern Europe. One can search in vain among Bulgarian and Hungarian films, while Rumania does in fact have a few films that have a random connection with flying.

One of the few East German flying films was made in 1958 and was directed by Erich Engel. It was a sharply propagandistic effort entitled *GESCHWADER FLEDERMAUS (The Bat Squadron).* It shows how American civil aircraft helped the French forces during the Vietnamese war of liberation. They were responsible not only for the transport of medical supplies and the wounded, but they also carried military equipment and ammunition. In the end of the film the hero deserts his unit and joins the North Vietnamese liberation movement.

In Czechoslovakia there were few flying films other than the aforementioned *UNOS* (1952). However, it is possible to find a cou-

Polish actors Bogusz Bilewski and Krystyna Iwasziewicz are in the cast of HISTORIA JEDNEGO MYSLIWCA (1958) (The Story of a Fighter Plane).

ple made by one director—Cenek Duba. In 1952 he made a film about sailplaning called *VITEZNA KRIDLA (Winged Victory),* and in 1958 came *V6 RANO NA LETISTI (Six O'Clock at the Airport),* which was quickly followed by *LETISTE NEPRIJIMA (The Airport Is Closed)* (1959).

The Polish director Leopold Buczkowski made the first Polish film about flying as early as 1930. It was called *GWIAZDZISTA ESKADRA (Star Squadron).* It was based on a screenplay by the well-known Polish pilot and author Janusz Meissner. In 1964 Buczkowski made *PRZERWANY LOT (Interrupted Flight),* which dealt with the war. It was a sentimental tale about a Russian pilot's travail in German-occupied Poland.

This Polish director also made a film about sailplanes in 1950 entitled *PIERWSZU START (First Solo).* In 1955 he filmed another Janusz Meissner novel called *NIEBIESKIE DROGI (Blue Trails),* but he changed the title to *SPRAWA PILOTA MARESZA (The Pilot Maresz Affair).* Buczkowski, it seems, was a kind of Polish William Wellman or Howard Hawks.

Actually, it is rather astonishing that so few Polish films about flying are concerned with the Second World War, especially since so many films generally deal with this painful period in the country's history. Polish volunteers took part in the Battle of Britain, as was shown in the British film *THE BATTLE OF BRITAIN* (1969), where Polish pilots, their training barely completed, dashed daringly into the air battles against the German fighter pilots. Certain problems arose when, in the heat of battle, the eager Polish pilots forgot their English and spoke in their mother tongue. The British squadron leader's hair almost turned gray as he tried to understand the cacophony of Polish pouring through his earphones.

In fact, there is also a Polish film dealing with the participation of Polish flyers in the R.A.F. battles during the war. It is called *HISTORIA JEDNEGO MYSLIWCA (The Story of a Fighter Plane)* and is based on the memoirs of Stanislaw Skalski. It was directed by Hubert Drapella. The same director made another flying film in 1961 called *PREZECIWKO BOGOM (Toward the Gods).* The action occurred in a milieu of modern flying and contained a considerable number of psychological conflicts. However, it was considered a rather weak film and more or less destroyed this director's advancing career.

In the dramatic climax of EKIPAJZ (1979) (The Crew) *an inflight repair to a failing engine is attempted.*

We have now flown with films under the hot Spanish sun, over Italy and under the Tricolor. The blue/gold flag of Sweden has waved and we have glided on the red wings of the Soviet Union. What at first seemed unresearched and impenetrable—at least to this author—has, despite the difficulties, found its way into print, the purpose of which has been to give the reader a balanced survey of events in other film skies.

THIS

Jet Progress and CinemaScope

Robert Stack in the Korean epic SABRE JET (1953).

At last, peace came to the movie screen. War films turned up now and then, but movie-makers and audiences were more interested in vast spectaculars.

A man by the name of Henri Chretien worked for many years trying to develop a photographic lens that could "shrink" the picture on the film frame. The width of the film was the normal 35 mm but the developed picture could be shown in an ordinary projector and with the aid of a special projection lens could be spread out over a much wider screen.

"Wide screen" was introduced. Fox, the first company to take advantage of the new system named it CinemaScope, which subsequently became synonymous with the wide-screen film system. Many other similar lenses have been developed through the years, like Panavision, SuperScope and WarnerScope, but CinemaScope seems to have become the best recognized name.

The film in which Fox introduced this system was *The Robe,* in 1953, and in it Richard Burton played his second starring role in Hollywood.

Wide screen not only gave a new screen depth to films but also brought with it a new dimension in sound: stereophonic sound. By hearing a multichannel optical sound system, the audience was treated to a new sensation in sound: a train was heard approaching at a distance on the left and after a few moments the locomotive and railway tracks roared deafeningly across the screen to fade out in the distance again on the right.

There were many wide-screen films made during the fifties. Besides *The Robe* (1953) there were such well-known movies as *Twenty Thousand Leagues Under The Sea* (1954), *The Ten Commandments* (1956), *Moby Dick* (1956), *The Bridge on the River Kwai* (1957) and *Ben-Hur* (1959).

But there were few flying films that used this new system, although it must be an almost perfect medium for capturing the freedom above the clouds.

Black Clouds From Eternity

Despite the fact that they were now facing the promising 1950s, film producers continued to try to squeeze more adventure and drama from a source that certainly should have been left dry for a long time.

In 1951 we were taken back to the archipelago of the South Pacific with a story in which John Wayne appeared as a tough squadron leader. It was called *FLYING LEATHERNECKS,* produced by RKO and Howard Hughes and directed by Nicholas Ray.

Wayne is the leader of a squadron of Grumman Hellcats belonging to the U.S. Marines. His deputy is Robert Ryan. This latter displays a certain indecisiveness and lack of fortitude, and Wayne, who is also his best friend, is reluctant to give him a squadron of his own. A conflict arises between the two men and soon develops into open hostility. But by the end of the film they are friends again and Ryan is given his own squadron to go on with the air battles above the wide Pacific and its jungle-covered islands.

FLYING LEATHERNECKS was a relatively good flying film from a number of points of view. There was, of course, much "we're the greatest" type of bombast, but this was overcome intermittently by the psychological conflict between the two men and the highly convincing battle scenes. The aerial photography and air battles were all first class. There was a lot of authentic documentary material used in the battle scenes and the relatively new "back-projection system" produced the convincing illusion for the audience that they were flying in the midst of an air battle.

The Battle of Britain formed the background for the story of a young R.A.F. pilot officer, "Septic" Baird (John Gregson), who joins a Hurricane squadron under the com-

John Wayne in FLYING LEATHERNECKS (1951).

Richard Todd as Squadron Leader Guy Gibson in the British story THE DAM BUSTERS (1954).

mand of Jack Hawkins. The film was called *ANGELS ONE FIVE* and was released in 1952. "Angels one five" stands for "enemy approaching at 15,000 feet." It was not a great film but, like most things produced by the British, it was well made and well played; it was directed by George More O'Ferrall.

A brief synopsis: "Septic" has problems with flying; he is afraid and unsure of himself. In addition to this, he is also having trouble being accepted by his colleagues, he is not really welcomed into the group. Some of them consider him to be weak and unreliable. The squadron leader is a tough officer who requires a great deal of his men. The times are very hard and the R.A.F. cannot afford to have any "bad" pilots. However, he believes the new young recruit to be made of sterner stuff and pays him a little extra attention—and look what happens! "Septic" suddenly becomes an accepted member of the squadron and is soon "one of the few" to whom so many owed so much. It does not have the happiest of endings—but perhaps the most logical one. "Septic" is shot down during an air battle and is killed.

Let us go back again to the Pacific, the background location of *FLAT TOP,* made by Monogram in 1952 and directed by Lesley Selander. Seen in the leading roles were Sterling Hayden, Richard Carlson, Keith Larsen and William Phipps. *FLAT TOP* was about life on board an aircraft carrier and life in the air above the Philippine Islands. The best part of the film was the description of how these gigantic floating airfields function, how men live and work in a milieu that breathes seamanship, oil, petrol, sweat and tears, where between times they come face to face with death under highly dramatic circumstances. There is always a certain drama in takeoffs and landings even when nothing actually "happens," and much of this drama is conveyed in the film, which was otherwise a rather weak story with a certain documentary value.

Also in 1952 came *THE WILD BLUE YONDER* from Republic. This dealt with the training of B-29 pilots and the bombing of Japan in the final phase of the war. Allan Dwan held the strings and appearing in the film were Wendell Corey, Forrest Tucker and Vera Ralston.

The very last bombing raids on the Japanese empire were depicted in 1952 in *ABOVE AND BEYOND.* In this film Metro-Goldwyn-Mayer told the tale of Colonel Paul Tibbets, his crew and the crews of the other bombers, who were all handpicked to carry out the most secret of all secret operations during the Second World War.

Tibbets (Robert Taylor) was given the task of training a squadron of B-29 pilots to carry a "very heavy" cargo of bombs from an island in the Pacific. The weight of the cargo

Like a real victor—"Septic" Baird (John Gregson) is carried aloft after he downed his first "Hun." From the British ANGELS ONE FIVE (1952).

Forrest Tucker (in black cap) gives his B-29 crew a briefing before takeoff. Far away in center: Wendell Corey. From THE WILD BLUE YONDER (1952).

was the only information they received and they trained with loads of ten-ton bombs on board their aircraft. Tibbets himself was the only person slated for the mission who knew what the real cargo would be. The target was also a secret. The crew was not briefed as to the real target and load until a few hours before takeoff. During this briefing they were also shown the first test explosion in the New Mexico desert, which had taken place on July 16.

Tibbets took off in his B-29, *Enola Gay* (his mother's name), from the island of Tinian in the Marianas at 2:45 A.M. on August 6, 1945. They learned when they were in the air that they would have three alternative targets depending on the weather (the planned alternative targets were: Hiroshima, Kokura and Nagasaki). Because of bad weather over most of Japan on that particular morning, the choice became Hiroshima which basked under an almost clear sky.

At 9:10 A.M. they approached their target, the bomb doors were opened, and at exactly 9:15 the bomb was dropped from *Enola Gay* and fell towards the earth of Japan. The sky above Japan remained clear only for a few seconds more. Everyone knows the rest of the story—and also that a second bomb was dropped on Nagasaki on the morning of August 8.

The development of the atomic bomb (Manhattan Project) and the final moment when it fell unquestionably comprise dramatic material for the filmmaker. And Norman Panama, who directed this semi-documentary, succeeded to some extent in giving a true picture of what happened and how the people involved reacted to one of the greatest misdeeds in the history of mankind.

Robert Taylor gave one of the best performances of his career as Tibbets and was helped by a number of other good players such as James Whitmore and Eleanor Parker (as Tibbets' wife).

Despite the romantic framework in which these real events were shown, I regard *ABOVE AND BEYOND* as one of the few ex-

Eleanor Parker and Robert Taylor (as Colonel Tibbets) in the MGM film ABOVE AND BEYOND (1952).

amples where the United States displayed a sense of guilt in relation to the bombings during those August days in 1945. I also see it as a good complement to the earlier film on the "Manhattan Project," *THE BEGINNING OR THE END* from 1948.

In *THE MALTA STORY* (1953), Alec Guinness portrayed a young reconnaissance pilot. Playing opposite him were Jack Hawkins, Anthony Steel and Muriel Pavlow. Malta's spirit of resistance was conveyed in this rather pale story about an introverted but brave Spitfire pilot who makes the final great sacrifice in the last few minutes of the film. It was shot on location in Malta and showed flying by Spitfires and Wellington bombers; it was directed by Brian Desmond Hurst.

In *THE DAM BUSTERS* (1954), the public was able to see an exciting and interesting depiction of the almost legendary bombing attacks on the dams at Möhn and Eder in the Ruhr Valley. It was directed by Michael Anderson, with Richard Todd (as Wing Commander Guy Gibson) and Michael Redgrave (as Barnes Wallis). The screenplay was based on Guy Gibson's book *Enemy Coast Ahead* which describes the whole planning of the operation and the attack—through the development and construction of Wallis' ingenious "bouncing bombs" to the completion of the attack on the night of May 16, 1943.

A still from THE DAM BUSTERS (1954). *Observe the enlarged bomb bay and the bouncing bomb of Mr. Wallis. The aircraft are Avro Lancasters.*

The tension is sustained right up to the exciting moment through the low-altitude night training flights and to the final approach on the target, when the daring pilots succeed in their goal—to blow up the big dams, thereby creating a severe power shortage for the enemy. Real Lancaster bombers were used in the film and, in addition, authentic sequences were included of test drops from a Mosquito light bomber.

THE SEA SHALL NOT HAVE THEM (1954) was a British film about sea rescue during the war. An R.A.F. Lockheed Hudson makes a forced landing at sea. There are a number of passengers on board besides the crew. One of these passengers is an air marshal played

Jack Hawkins briefs his personnel in the British THE MALTA STORY (1953).

by Michael Redgrave. The pilot manages to bring the plane down more or less in one piece and all the crew and passengers succeed in getting out of the sinking aircraft and into a rubber lifeboat. We then see how the rescue operation functions both in the air and at sea, and the castaways are eventually picked up in a fast lifeboat.

The usual excellent performances by British actors were given by Dirk Bogarde, Nigel Patrick, Anthony Steel, Jack Watling and others. Lewis Gilbert directed it and the R.A.F., Royal Navy and Coastal Command cooperated to provide authentic background.

Before we leave the bombing raids and air battles of the Second World War and enter the jet age, let us linger a moment more in the epoch of the propellor and consider yet another film about "the few" to whom so much was owed.

It was the Rank Organisation that gave us *REACH FOR THE SKY* (1956), a film biography of British fighter pilot Douglas Bader. It was based on Paul Brickhill's book which told about Bader from the beginning of his training in 1928 to his tragic crash during a flying exhibition in which he lost both his legs. The film continued from·there showing

Anthony Steel (left) and Alec Guinness in THE MALTA STORY (1953).

The crew escape their sinking Lockheed Hudson. From the left: Jack Watling, Dirk Bogarde, Bonar Colleano and, in the dinghy, Michael Redgrave. From the film THE SEA SHALL NOT HAVE THEM (1954).

his rehabilitation and the force of his will as he learned to walk and dance again, and also to fly.

Bader, excellently portrayed by Kenneth More, succeeded in everything he attempted and the audience was able to see how he hounded the Ministry of Air to allow him to reenter the service as a fighter pilot.

The year was 1939 and eight years had elapsed since his crash. He flew his Hurricane under official protest but there was apparently no one in the squadron who claimed that he was a bad pilot. He was a wonderful flyer and was among the top aces during the Battle of Britain. He is ranked as 16th among R.A.F. aces. When he was shot down over enemy territory in 1941, he had twenty-three scores to his credit. There would certainly have been more if he had succeeded in any of his attempts to escape from the German prisoner-of-war camps he was forced to remain in until the end of the war.

All this is in the film and it is charmingly and accurately told by Lewis Gilbert. A curious fact is that when Bader was shot down he was at first unable to get out of the cockpit as the plane plummeted toward earth, but managed to at the last moment by unfastening one of his artificial legs, which crashed with the aircraft while Bader parachuted to safety. His right leg was found in the demolished plane. When he was a prisoner of the Germans, they permitted a British aircraft to fly over and drop a new set of legs for him—a gesture that sounds almost too chivalrous to believe but it is in fact true.

Top left: Bader's Bristol "Bulldog" after the fatal crash of 1931. Center: "Bader's Bus Gang" on alert during The Battle of Britain (with book and smoking pipe: Kenneth More as Bader). Bottom: Scramble! All pilots rush on to their planes. Bader himself makes it easily due to his artificial legs. From REACH FOR THE SKY (1956).

Kenneth More gave a very good portrait of Bader and here you can see him jump down from his Hurricane after a successful mission. From REACH FOR THE SKY (1956).

Higher—and Faster than Sound

By the end of the 1940s the jet engine had passed out of the experimental years and had become more common as the source of power in fighter aircraft. It would still be some time before it was used in civilian airplanes.

Before the end of hostilities, the German aircraft industry had a couple of jet-powered aircraft in service in their squadrons. They functioned satisfactorily and were an unpleasant surprise for Allied bomber and fighter pilots. One of these aircraft was the Messerschmitt Me 262 which was completely jet powered, whereas the small "flying wing" Me 163 Komet was rocket powered and had a very short range. Both these aircraft were put into service in late 1944 but, because of a mistake made by Hitler, the Me 262 was used largely as a bomber—a mistake that must be counted lucky for the Allies.

Some picture material is preserved of these unique aircraft in operation, taken by war photographers who went along on Allied bombing missions. One sequence is included in Warners' *CHAIN LIGHTNING* (1950). This film was directed by Stuart Heisler and starred Humphrey Bogart as Matt Brennan, a former bomber pilot who tries after the war to make a living as an aeronautical acrobat. At a party he meets an old flying companion who introduces him to Willis (Raymond Massey), an industrial magnate. The latter hires Matt as a test pilot at his aircraft factory.

Matt's duties are to look after the tests of a new jet fighter made in Willis' factory in the hope that they will land a contract with the U.S. Air Force. The designer of the plane, whose name is Troxell (Richard Whorf), wants Matt to wait before carrying out the final tests. He has not completed the ejection cockpit to his own satisfaction. Willis, however, is eager to introduce his aircraft to the military authorities and succeeds in talking

Humphrey Bogart as test pilot Matt Brennan in CHAIN LIGHTNING (1949).

Nigel Patrick and a model of the leading aircraft in THE SOUND BARRIER (1952).

Matt into making a long-planned record flight over the North Pole without the ejection system.

Matt completes the flight and breaks all speed and altitude records. The military is delighted and Willis rubs his hands in satisfaction. But everything becomes clouded when Troxell himself makes the first test of the ejection equipment. Something goes wrong and he is killed. Matt, who feels partly responsible for Troxell's death, busies himself in work to complete his friend's invention, which despite its initial failure represents a revolutionary idea—instead of the pilot being catapulted out with his seat, which involves considerable risk of injury, Troxell's idea is to have the whole nose section of the plane rocketed free and then drift down in a parachute. In this way the pilot would be completely protected from injury due to the great speed.

Top right: From CHAIN LIGHTNING (1949). *Center: From* APPOINTMENT IN LONDON (1952). *Dirk Bogarde gives his men a briefing about the target for the night.*

The exciting climax of the film is reached when Matt takes off to carry out the final test in the ejection capsule. Everyone involved watches and waits expectantly from the ground, including Jo Halloway (Eleanor Parker), Willis' secretary who is in love with Matt and has had an affair with him earlier during the war. Matt flies very high and fast and presses the button to release the cabin. Everything functions perfectly and a big parachute carries the ejected cabin safely to earth. Willis can now sign the military contract and Matt and Jo can sign their marriage licence. Happy ending—once again!

The following year, 1951, it was Universal's turn to show what jet flight was all about. Joseph Pevney directed *AIR CADET*, with Stephen McNally, Gail Russell, Charles Drake, Richard Long and Alex Nicol in the main roles. This film concerned the training of jet pilots for the American Air Force and was a thin, dull tale about the problems young pilot cadets have with their flying and their instructor. One of them even gets tangled up with the instructor's wife, an understanding little woman who sees to it that everything is straightened out in time for the magnificent flying display by the famous Acro Jets. In fact these pilots, with their F-80 Shooting Stars, played some of the leading

Bottom right, from left: James Best, Alex Nicol, Charles Drake, Gail Russell, Stephen McNally, Richard Long and Robert Arthur in AIR CADET (1951).

Matt Brennan in a romantic meeting with his love Jo Halloway (Eleanor Parker). He has just landed safely with the rescue capsule. From CHAIN LIGHTNING (1949).

roles in the excellent flying scenes. The film was a big propaganda number for the U.S.A.F. and fulfilled the desire of the cinema-going flying enthusiast for action in the air.

In 1952, the British released *APPOINTMENT IN LONDON,* with Dirk Bogarde, Bryan Forbes and Dinah Sheridan. Bogarde gave his usual brilliant performance as a war-weary and dutiful bomber squadron leader. There were not too many flying sequences, but they were dramatic and well made.

One of the best film tales from the fifties also came from Britain. Its title: *THE SOUND BARRIER* (1952). Terence Rattigan wrote the screenplay and London Films recruited one of England's best filmmakers, David Lean, to direct it. I personally found it a very poetic and interesting story about test flying and a new jet aircraft. Some of the most competent actors in Great Britain at the time appeared in it: Sir Ralph Richardson, Nigel Patrick, Ann Todd, John Justin and Dinah Sheridan.

A brief summary: a British aircraft manufacturer (Richardson) hires his daughter's fiancé, Tony (Patrick), as a test pilot at his aircraft works. Tony is a former R.A.F. fighter pilot and is considered very competent. He is made head of a project for a new fighter. The aircraft is already built and he begins a series of flight tests. He also brings an old friend (Justin) into the company. He marries his boss's daughter (Todd) and they live a happy but hectic life together. But when their first child arrives, Tony's wife begins to suffer fears about the dangerous work.

Certain aerodynamic problems have developed. Only with great difficulty is it possible to pull the aircraft out of steep, high-speed dives. In other words, the diving angle becomes steeper as the speed increases.

Tony has a good working relationship with the head designer, but occasionally he displays a certain lack of imagination. On the other hand, Tony's friend, who is as good a pilot as he is himself, has an idea how to solve the problem, but Tony refuses to listen.

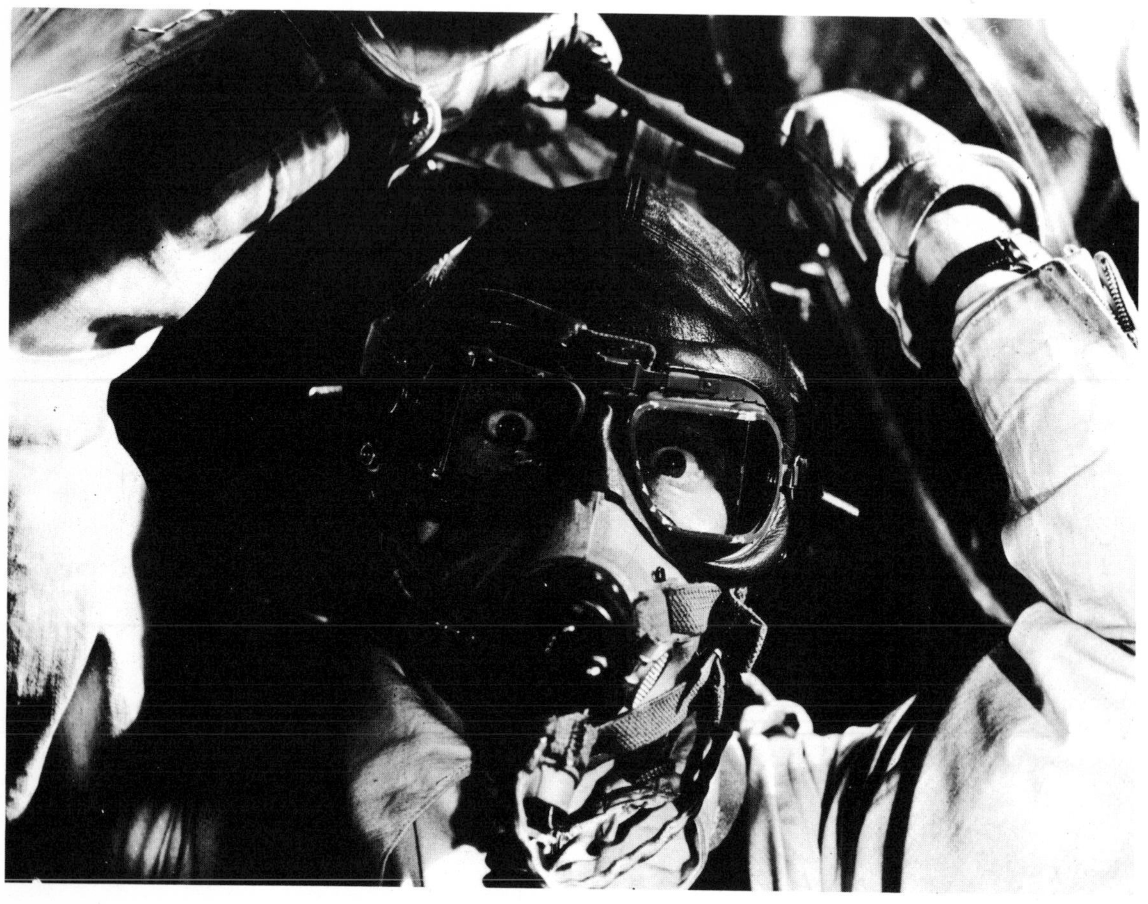

From THE SOUND BARRIER (1952). Nigel Patrick, as the test pilot Tony, in "the moment of truth." His decision to eject is too late and he is killed when his Supermarine Swift crashes into the ground.

He believes that it should be possible to exceed the magic Mach 1.0 (Mach 1.0 = speed of sound at sea level at 15° C = 1,125 kilometers per hour).

Tony takes off for the final test and climbs to maximum altitude. He makes a couple of preliminary dives and finds that the aircraft, as usual, becomes nose heavy at a speed of approximately Mach 0.95. It vibrates violently and is difficult to pull out of the dive. But Tony is determined. He climbs once again to maximum altitude and in an almost totally vertical dive he plummets toward the shimmering, misty earth. The altimeter and airspeed indicator spin wildly, the mach meter shows 0.95. The aircraft begins to vibrate violently and the needle passes the 0.97 mark, but height is rapidly reduced and Tony must start to pull out of the dive. But the plane is no longer under control, the stick is immovable and the dive becomes ever steeper. He takes hold of the catapult release intending to eject—but it is too late, and in the final fraction of a second he realizes that he has solved the problem but lost everything.

There is a heavy gloom after the crash, of course, but the show must go on. Now Tony's friend has to take over and at last it is he and the designer together who solve the mystery of the heavy nose section. The tail section is simply too fragile. In pulling out of the dive the aircraft bends out of shape through the enormous stresses on the surface of the tail fins. The elevator effect is completely reversed—instead of bringing the plane out of the dive, just the opposite happens with catastrophic effects. In the end, a solution is found and the beautiful aircraft—Supermarine Swift—is certified by the R.A.F. and goes into production.

From a technical point of view, *THE SOUND BARRIER* must be ranked among the top ten films about flying; it was highly interesting in its description of the aerodynamic problems mentioned previously. Lively discussions were held among people in the field as to whether the problem described in the film was credible or not. In fact, it was. The problem was real enough at the time—the late 1940s—and still constituted an unknown factor in the understanding of aerodynamics and an almost insurmountable obstacle in breaking the so-called sound barrier. The mystery was solved and the sound barrier was broken for the first time on October 14, 1947, by the American test pilot Charles E. Yeager in a Bell X-1. The following year the British also passed the magic mark.

Supermarine Swift from THE SOUND BARRIER (1952).

THE SOUND BARRIER overshadowed a well-made and exciting flying thriller called *THE NET* (1953). The highly talented Anthony Asquith directed the British production, which starred James Donald, Phyllis Calvert, Herbert Lom and Noel William.

The action takes place at a secret air base where a sensational new jet plane is being tested. The X-7 has attracted wide interest,

John Hodiak wishes Guy Madison good luck before a parachute test from very high altitude (100,000 ft./ 31,000 m). From the Fox movie ON THE THRESHOLD OF SPACE (1955).

From left: Murray Hamilton, Lloyd Nolan, unknown player and William Holden in the Warner test flight drama TOWARD THE UNKNOWN (1956).

particularly from Eastern Europe. A secret agent infiltrates the test team and joins the designer on a flight. With the mission successfully completed, the pilot sets his course for home, but a revolver is put to his head. Told to turn the plane eastward, he struggles and the plane dives out of control. The hero regains consciousness in time to avoid a crash, but the villain has suffocated.

ON THE THRESHOLD OF SPACE (1956) dealt with other experiments in flying research and medical research related to flying. It was produced by Fox and concerned a high-altitude balloon flight and free falling at high speeds and high-altitude parachute jumps. Robert D. Webb, who directed this film, shot most of it at Holoman and Eglin air bases in Florida, where much of the experimental equipment used in the film was located.

The person on whom the leading character was based was Colonel Stapp, an Air Force doctor who carried out a series of tests on the acceleration tolerance of the human body (G-force). He subjected himself to enormous strains and was once thrust forward at a speed of 1,600 kilometers per hour in a rocket-powered sled to see whether the human body could withstand the rapid deceleration without injury. He made it! But not entirely without injury. Stapp had to be treated afterwards for severe hemorrhaging and eye injuries. This and much else could be witnessed in this scientifically accurate and exciting film about research into flying.

The leading roles were played by Guy Madison, John Hodiak, Dean Jagger and Virginia Leith. The high point of the film, literally, comes when Madison and a colleague climb to 100,000 feet in a balloon and then parachute to earth. He free-falls down to 15,000 feet before opening his parachute and drifting to safety once again on mother earth. Talk about drama! But this actually happened in real life and fortunately was filmed in color with a number of cameras.

After the breaking of the sound barrier, there came a virtual landslide in development. Charles Yeager broke his own record in 1951 when he reached 1,555 km/h and by 1956 Milburn Apt achieved the incredible speed of 3,370 km/h. But this was 1956—and it would not be long before even greater speeds were reached. But let us linger for a moment with the Bell X-2, the aircraft that played an important role in Warners' interesting and very dramatic *TOWARD THE UNKNOWN* (1956).

In this film William Holden played a former fighter pilot from the Korean War who returns home and begins working with test flights of rocket-powered aircraft at Edwards Air Force Base. It primarily concerned the Bell X-1 and X-2, but there were also a num-

Charles Bronson as a tough test flyer in X-15 (1961).

William Holden cleared for release from the mother ship in his Bell X-2. From TOWARD THE UNKNOWN (1956).

ber of other airplanes involved.

The building of the aircraft was followed in great detail: how the technical and aerodynamic problems arose and how they were eventually solved, until finally the goal was achieved—to fly higher and faster than ever before. Holden, who was at the apex of his career at the time, gave a good portrayal of a highly competent, thoughtful test pilot; Lloyd Nolan and Virginia Leith also appeared in important roles. The film was directed by veteran Mervyn LeRoy and it is included in this author's list of favorites.

It is not until 1961 that we can once again see altitude and speed records broken in the cinema. In that year Major Robert White reached a speed of 4,675 km/h in a North American X-15. The X-15, built entirely of steel, achieved its absolute maximum speed of 7,297 km/h in 1967.

United Artists made a film about this fantastic aircraft, directed by Richard D. Donner and called simply *X-15*. Unfortunately, despite remarkable aerial photography, the film must be regarded as too light to deserve recommendation. Not even Charles Bronson, relatively unknown at the time, was able to show much enthusiasm for his part as a test pilot, nor was the rest of the cast more convincing. They included David McLean, James Gregory, Mary Tyler Moore and Patricia Owens.

An interesting fact is that the X-15 also holds the altitude record for fixed-wing aircraft. This record is 107,960 meters and was set by Joseph A. Walker in 1963. It is not really possible to fly much faster or higher with ordinary or out-of-the-ordinary aircraft. The time has come for new goals to be set—outer space itself and its unknown, infinitely distant galaxies.

ORAL INFLATION
CONNECTOR LOOP
EQUIPMENT

War over the 38th Parallel

In June 1950, North Korean troops attacked South Korea. A new war was now a fact. The United States intervened immediately and the U.N. Security Council, which declared North Korea the aggressor, mobilized a U.N. force under American leadership with the purpose of restoring order in the country. The Soviet Union did not participate in the U.N. resolution. North Korea had China as an ally and later received military aid from the Soviets.

The 38th parallel became the mystical frontier and it was crossed by U.N. forces under General Douglas MacArthur in September 1950. China issued a warning against further advances but this was ignored by MacArthur. China attacked and drove the U.N. forces back beyond the 38th parallel.

Seoul, the capital of South Korea, fell into Communist hands a couple of times before the U.N. forces were able to mount a successful counterattack. Eventually the front line was stabilized at the 38th parallel and in July 1953 a truce was signed. The truce has subsequently been guaranteed by the U.N. Truce Commission and representatives of both the North and South Korean governments. The Korean War was a very bloody conflict in which the North lost approximately two million men and the South one million.

The war gave Hollywood filmmakers, of course, no peace either—here was a new field of operations which could be exploited to the limit. Despite the horror of the subject, there were in fact some rather good films made depicting this latest hell on earth. There were also many more mediocre movies of a purely speculative nature.

Samuel Fuller's *THE STEEL HELMET* (1950) and *FIXED BAYONETS* (1951) were both films of the better type. Fuller's idea was to try to show just exactly how war is. There was neither romance nor endless heroics. The only thing the soldiers met on the battlefield was blood, sweat and death, in *close*, so why not let the movie audience do the same?

There were, of course, a lot of purely commercial productions, but, with the making of *SUBMARINE COMMAND* (1951), John Farrow showed that there were decent exceptions. Another exception was Richard Brooks's *BATTLE CIRCUS* (1952), but the fact is that good films about this war were very thin on the ground.

It is a pleasure to note that there were a number of films about flying from the period and that a couple of these raised the average quality above the level mentioned above.

They began modestly in 1953 with *DRAGONFLY SQUADRON*. It was produced by Allied Artists and had in the main roles John Hodiak, Bruce Bennett, Jess Parker and Barbara Britton, and was directed by Lesley Selander. It concerned one of the first fighter squadrons sent into battle in Korea, which

A North American P-51 Mustang flashes across the airfield in DRAGONFLY SQUADRON (1953).

Mickey Rooney as the helicopter rescuer Mike Forney in THE BRIDGES AT TOKO-RI (1954). *Behind Rooney, a glimpse of his crew buddy "Nestor," played by Earl Holliman.*

flew the slightly obsolete propeller-driven North American P-51 Mustang.

In *SABRE JET* (1953), United Artists displayed more modern aircraft. Louis King directed this effort and let Robert Stack and Richard Arlen fly around in brand new F-86s, or Sabres, as they came to be known. Coleen Gray beautified the milieu for Stack and Arlen but King failed, although the air battles were filled with action and speed and well done, to make a really successful film about flying.

A new method of mounting cameras on aircraft was used in this film. They were mounted in such a way that wide-angle lenses could be attached to the tip of the fins and aimed forward. Thus, the audience got the impression that they themselves were participating in the actual battle or that they were really maneuvering the very fast jets in for a landing on the concrete runway.

In another film from 1953 we were able to see the small unit aircraft that the U.S. Army operated at the front line, usually in artillery reconnaissance or as ambulances to transport the wounded to field hospitals. The film was called *MISSION OVER KOREA;* it was directed by Fred F. Sears and starred John Derek, John Hodiak and Audrey Totter.

In 1954 came *BATTLE TAXI.* This was

Barbara Britton and John Hodiak in DRAGONFLY SQUADRON (1953).

John Derek in Fred F. Sears' MISSION OVER KOREA (1953). *Behind Derek we can see Harvey Lembeck.*

about helicopter pilots whose job it was to rescue pilots who had been shot down or crashed in Korea—on both sides of the enemy lines, or far out to sea. Appearing in this excellent tale about the daily routine of war were Sterling Hayden, Marshall Thompson and Arthur Franz. This movie could almost be characterized as a feature-length instruction film. There were moments when it provided a thrilling picture of how the wounded are rescued from the front line and how pilots who have parachuted out of their aircraft are fished out of the sea. Herbert L. Strock made this slightly different film for United Artists—very acceptable!

In *MEN OF THE FIGHTING LADY,* Andrew Marton showed the contribution of an aircraft carrier during a battle among the islands off the Asiatic coast. It was made in 1954 by Metro and starred Van Johnson, Dewey Martin, Walter Pidgeon and Keenan Wynn.

We were able to follow a number of jet pilots during their attacks and air battles. The screenplay was based on James A. Michener's *Forgotten Heroes of Korea* and *The Case of the Blind Pilot* by Commander Harry A. Burns. The main theme of the latter book also comprised the main action of the film, which was otherwise a rather simple story—more about machines than men. An exception to this was Keenan Wynn's performance as a pilot who is getting "too old" and who is aware of his growing limitations—a fine portrayal of a cynical and tragic man. He is subsequently killed, due to his inability to judge his speed and height correctly, while trying to land his aircraft. The actual crash was in fact the real thing: the aircraft was a McDonnell Banshee and the pilot survived the crash without injury, which seems little short of a miracle when you actually see it for yourself.

The high point of the film, however, comes in a dramatic scene when Van Johnson, by flying very close to another plane, helps a pilot friend who has been blinded to land his aircraft on the deck of the carrier. It was very exciting and the audience held its breath until the wounded pilot, after a couple of at-

tempts, managed to land his Grumman Cougar on the undulating flight deck. This situation occurred in reality but it was during the Second World War. The blind pilot was then flying a Grumman Hellcat and was helped by another pilot to make a belly landing on a beach in the Pacific.

In 1954 Paramount made one of their so-called "spectaculars." This was Mark Robson's *THE BRIDGES AT TOKO-RI.* Robson succeeded here, not just in making a first-class film about flying but a remarkably good film by any standard, a film that deserves a more detailed description.

Once again it was about carrier-based aircraft sent out on missions against North Korea. William Holden played Harry Brubaker, a young Lieutenant who had not asked to fight but found himself right in the middle of the conflict. He is torn between his duty and love for his wife and children. He is a calm, competent pilot, and his commander, "Cag" (Charles McGraw), would like to give him a squadron of his own. The head of operations, Admiral Tarrant (Fredric March), sees in Brubaker a carbon copy of his own son, who was killed in the war, and therefore keeps himself well-informed about Brubaker's actions and attitudes. On one occasion Brubaker is forced to belly-land his Grumman Panther in the sea and is fished up in a helicopter by Mike Forney (Mickey Rooney). Forney is a little character (excellently played by Rooney) who, in defiance of instructions, flies about wearing a green top hat and an equally bright green "Richthofen scarf." He knows that his buddies "down there in the drink" feel absolutely safe when they spot his green attire.

After returning from leave where he has seen his wife (Grace Kelly) and two small daughters, Harry becomes even more repelled by what he is doing—partly he hates shooting at people and partly he is simply afraid of dying.

The squadron is faced with a very difficult and dangerous assignment—they are to bomb the well-fortified bridges at Toko-Ri. Everyone in the squadron is aware that some of them will not return from the raid.

Brubaker goes along with his commander in an attempt to get photographs of the target. Afterwards, when he relives the sight of Cag running the gauntlet through the deep ravine leading to the bridges, he has a nervous collapse. He recovers control of himself, however, and when the squadron is ready to take off from the flight deck for the attack he is sitting in his aircraft waiting to be catapulted into the air.

Because of the photographs Cag managed to get of the target on their earlier reconnaissance mission, the attack is a success beyond all expectations. The bridges are destroyed

From THE BRIDGES AT TOKO-RI (1954). *William Holden (lower left) crouches down under cover of a ditch. An enemy patrol has surrounded his belly-landed Panther.*

Blinded during a mission, Dewey Martin crash-lands his Grumman F9F Cougar aboard an aircraft carrier with help from his section buddy, played by Van Johnson. THE MEN OF THE FIGHTING LADY (1954).

Both stills on this page from THE BRIDGES AT TOKO-RI (1954).

Right: Harry Brubaker (Holden) and Mike Forney (Rooney) scramble for cover after the enemy has destroyed Forney's chopper and killed his friend "Nestor." Below: Forney and Brubaker in one of the last dramatic scenes of the film. They know they are doomed but decided to "try to the last . . ." One minute later they are both dead.

with a minimum of losses. But on the return flight Harry discovers that he is losing fuel. When his comrades check his aircraft underneath, they report that his plane has been hit and fuel is leaking out.

His life-sustaining fuel leaks quickly away and Harry tries to fly over the mountains to the sea where he knows that he can receive help when he parachutes out. When the engine finally stops, the mountains are still far ahead of him and he realizes that he is too low to glide over the high peaks. He rejects the idea of jumping since he knows that the enemy usually shoots parachutists, and chooses instead to belly-land his Panther in a field. He lands without injury and dashes from his burning plane to hide in a nearby ditch. However, the enemy have seen him crash-land and he is soon surrounded by a patrol. A group of attack planes tries to help him by attacking the patrol but are finally forced to leave because of a shortage of fuel.

Harry Brubaker, a twenty-nine-year-old lawyer from Denver, Colorado, now finds himself all alone in a country that he never thought he would have to defend. And certainly not in a war which he fails completely to understand.

Everything seems to be over for Brubaker when suddenly Mike Forney comes clattering along in his rescue helicopter. It is rather like the old matinee westerns when the calvary arrived—shouts of relief and joy! The maker of the film had, however, not considered such a simple end. The helicopter is hit by Communist fire and put out of action. Mike is forced to hide in the ditch with Harry. They make up their minds to hold out until help arrives. But the North Koreans greatly outnumber them. Forney is killed first by a hand grenade, and then Brubaker is overcome, shot and then bayoneted.

Despite the shocking violence and brutality of the end, it seems in some way to be the logical conclusion to the story. When the camera moves away from Brubaker's twisted body in the muddy ditch—so far from the security of shipboard—the huge war ship fades in as it steams forward far out in the storm-lashed sea.

Again, the screenplay was based on a novel of James A. Michener, for which he received the famous Pulitzer Prize. It was a best seller in America, not the least for its unusually honest and straightforward view of the meaningless conflict in Korea. In the film version, too, which followed the book closely, Robson's direction achieved an authentic, almost pacifist atmosphere even though there were some elements of "we're the greatest" bombast—after all, the U.S. Navy had contributed to making a film out of Michener's remarkable story. One has to expect a little propaganda. We must also mention that *THE BRIDGES OF TOKO-RI* received an Oscar for the best technical effects in 1954.

During 1955 there were a couple of further films made about airborne seamen. One was *AIR STRIKE* from Lippert Pictures, with Richard Denning and Don Haggerthy. Another was *AN ANNAPOLIS STORY* with John Derek, Diana Lynn and Kevin McCarthy. The second of these films was about the training of jet pilots in the American fleet and was produced by Allied Artists and directed by Don Siegel.

Warners also produced a Korean film in 1955. The point of this film was to tell the story of the American air ace Joseph McConnell and was called *THE McCONNELL STORY*. It was directed by Gordon Douglas and was the usual romanticized run of the mill stuff. The excellently filmed dogfights above the Yalu River between F-86 Sabres and the Russian-built Mig-15s (in the film represented by F-84F Thunderstreaks) never really had a chance to hold their own against the embraces between Alan Ladd (McConnell) and June Allyson (McConnell's wife). The only convincing performance in the film was by that solid actor James Whitmore who played a fighter pilot and McConnell's friend from flying school and the war years in Europe. (In actual fact Joseph McConnell was killed in a crash when carrying out a low-altitude, high-speed test flight in an F-86H.)

Josef von Sternberg—one of the all-time great directors and creator of *THE BLUE ANGEL* (1930)—found himself in a period of

From left we can see: Kevin McCarthy, John Derek, Pat Conway and Don Kennedy in AN ANNAPOLIS STORY (1955).

Alan Ladd and James Whitmore in THE McCONNELL STORY (1955).

Alan Ladd as the famous American jet fighter ace, Joseph McConnell. The plane is a Lockheed F-80 Shooting Star.

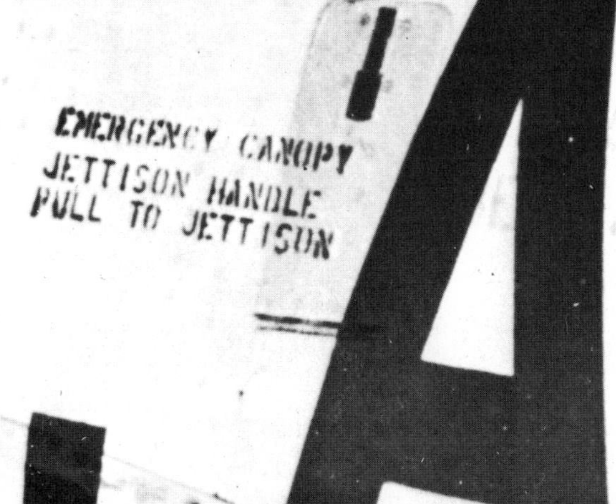

Josef von Sternberg's rubbishy JET PILOT *(1952) with Janet Leigh as a very beautiful Russian pilot seeking political asylum. Here she is examined by John Wayne and Jay C. Flippen (in the chair).*

THE HUNTERS (1958). *A Communist pilot on alert in his Mig. The aircraft type used as Migs are Republic F-84F Thunderstreaks.*

decline in the 1950s: he was driven to concoct a terrible stew for RKO called *JET PILOT*. It was a kind of *NINOTCHKA* of flying films: a female Soviet pilot (Janet Leigh) flies off course—perhaps intentionally—from Russia to Alaska. She is intercepted by an American jet fighter which escorts her to an American base. The pilot of the escorting aircraft (John Wayne) is also the person who is given the task of "taking care" of her, for the time being. They soon fall in love and she gets to enjoy everything in the wonderful capitalist world. But then she becomes homesick and wants to return to Russia. He gives in to her and goes along with her to Moscow. More regrets! They escape from the Soviets in a stolen jet plane and return again to the beautiful old capitalist United States, with its thick steaks and long drinks . . . .

Well, I would rather see *THE HUNTERS* (1958), directed by Dick Powell, which was a decent flying tale although no masterpiece. Powell made it for Fox and the cast included Robert Mitchum, Robert Wagner, May Britt, Richard Egan and Lee Philips. The romantic intrigue was excessively weak but the flying sequences were competently done. And this summary can apply to far too many of the films made against the background of the air battles over the 38th parallel and Yalu River.

John Gabriel (left) and Robert Mitchum in Dick Powell's Korean air war epic THE HUNTERS *(1958). Aircraft in the background are North American F-86 Sabres.*

17

The High and the Mighty

The above title will have to stand for a number of odd flying films released during the ten years between 1950 and 1960. Not all of them were about war even if many were played against a military background. There are also a couple of really good flying stories which belong in this section of our anthology.

The first two that appeared were based on books by Ernest K. Gann. Both were directed by our old friend William Wellman for Warners.

The first of these was *ISLAND IN THE SKY* (1953), with John Wayne playing the old veteran pilot Dooley. Flying his C-47 (DC 3), he is forced down in the wild and isolated tundra of Labrador. Despite the cold, the snow and privations, he succeeds in keeping his freezing, disconsolate crew together until help at last arrives.

It was an exciting film that provided good instruction for pilots who have crash-landed in the wilderness. The cast included Lloyd Nolan, Walter Abel, Andy Devine, Sean McClory and Hal Baylor.

Wellman's second film was entitled *THE HIGH AND THE MIGHTY* (1954). It was based on a best seller by Gann and told the story of a passenger plane on a flight from Honolulu to San Francisco. The aircraft was a four-engine Douglas DC-6 and its pilots were John Wayne and Robert Stack. Wayne played the old experienced pilot. He had been sitting in aircraft for over thirty years and was still, at a little over fifty, full of health and vitality. But he is not the captain any longer. An earlier crash, for which he was legally responsible, has deprived him of his place in the captain's seat on the left-hand side of the cockpit. Sitting there instead is Stack, a young and "unblemished" colleague. But when they are far out over the Pacific, strong headwinds slow them down and use up much of their fuel; it is then the older of the two "eagles" who coolly takes over and makes sure that they arrive in 'Frisco all in one piece.

John Wayne gave one of his best performances in this film, and the music by Dimitri Tiomkin became as popular as the melody he composed for *High Noon* (1952). Two compositions for which Tiomkin received Oscars.

Gann's book about pilots and their struggle to save their passengers, their aircraft and their own lives is a minor masterpiece, and William Wellman's film adaptation was done with a competent and steady hand. This excellent film about flying was produced by Warner Bros.

In 1954, the British reported in again with *OUT OF THE CLOUDS* from Ealing Studios, with Anthony Steel in the lead as the young airline pilot. Robert Beatty played a tough airport officer and James Robertson Justice a loud and loquacious old flight captain.

Although it had certain good qualities, *OUT OF THE CLOUDS* was not better than mediocre. However, a flying tale by Paramount in 1955 definitely was. This was *STRATEGIC AIR COMMAND* with James Stewart in the leading role as an American reserve officer and baseball star who is called up for reserve duty in the Strategic Bomber

Right: From ISLAND IN THE SKY (1953) *we can see Wally Cassell, John Wayne and Hal Baylor.*

Gary Cooper as "Billy" Mitchell in the air and courtroom drama THE COURT MARTIAL OF BILLY MITCHELL (1955). *The machine is a Curtiss Jenny.*

WARNER BROS. PRESENT
WILLIAM A. WELLMAN'S
"THE HIGH AND THE M
JOHN WAYNE · CLAIRE TREVOR · LARAINE DAY · ROBERT STACK · JAN STERLIN

John Wayne (right) as Dan Roman, the pilot who has used up all his "nine lives" and started on the tenth. From William Wellman's exciting and well-done air drama THE HIGH AND THE MIGHTY (1954). *At left, William Campbell and, in the middle, Robert Stack.*

Command. It was not difficult for Stewart to play this role. He had flown his twenty-five "tours" as skipper of a B-24 Liberator over Germany during the Second World War, so he knew how to act behind the controls and instruments of a bomber.

Under the excellent direction of Anthony Mann, this film became not merely an act of homage to the Strategic Air Command (S.A.C.) but also one of the most beautiful flying films ever made. The new VistaVision system showed magnificent scenes from the flyers' world—where high above the clouds the vapor trails from the B-36s and B-47s chalk a pattern across the endless ice-blue skies. There are many exciting moments, but the culmination comes when Stewart, after his one arm becomes lame (an old baseball injury), is forced to land his B-47 during terrible weather.

Anthony Steel in the British OUT OF THE CLOUDS (1954).

Top left: THE NIGHT MY NUMBER CAME UP (1955), *a British film not mentioned in the text. It was a flashback drama with, among others, Nigel Stock (left), Michael Redgrave and Victor Maddern (far right).*

Well made, instructive, it was also exciting—even for a professional who knows how difficult it can be to manipulate the throttle, elevators and landing gear control when the instruments are on the left and only the right hand is functioning.

Also in the cast was June Allyson as Stewart's wife, constant and close, with a blinding smile. Frank Lovejoy, Barry Sullivan and Alex Nicol gave support as friends and colleagues.

The American Colonel, William (Billy) Mitchell, was a bellicose man who tried for a long time before the war to convince the American government and the Department of Defense of the importance of a strong Air Force.

This was in the late 1920s and early 1930s. He finally succeeded, but not before he was pilloried in court and deprived of all his honors and rank. Otto Preminger used this dramatic material in *THE COURT MARTIAL OF BILLY MITCHELL* (1955) which he made for Warners. Gary Cooper was given the role of Mitchell. Cooper never gave a bad performance, and this role was no exception.

The most exciting moment in the film comes during the dramatic court-martial scene in which there are brilliant perfor-

A B-47 crew in preparedness for takeoff (facing page, lower left). From one of the best air movies from the fifties—STRATEGIC AIR COMMAND (1955).

mances by both Cooper and the prosecutor, played by Ralph Bellamy. (Bellamy, who worked with Warners in the thirties and who always played the "nice guy who never gets the girl," made a remarkable film comeback in this movie after having spent many years on the Broadway stage.)

The flying was somewhat downstaged but what there was of it was very good and provided some unique documentary sequences. It should be added that Mitchell predicted the Japanese attack on Pearl Harbor as early as 1923.

Then came a British film, *THE MAN IN THE SKY,* in 1956. This concerned an old pilot who has to make a forced landing in a Bristol Freighter because of engine trouble. Before he finally lands the plane, there are many exciting moments and in the end the aircraft catches on fire and burns up.

Another film in uniform: the uniform of the American Air Force to be precise. It was made by Warners in 1957 and called *BOMBERS B-52*. Karl Malden, Efrem Zimbalist, Jr., and Natalie Wood were directed by Gordon Douglas in this film about S.A.C. and the training of crews for the giant Boeing B-52 Stratofortresses. The photography was good but it had a barely acceptable story.

The British *HIGH FLIGHT* from the same year provided a much more positive surprise. This was the story of a flying-mad R.A.F. cadet who found it difficult to conform to military discipline. As a means of emphasizing his lack of respect for his superiors, he does dangerous acrobatics right before the eyes of the head of the training school, excellently played by Ray Milland. It is an old theme perhaps but surprisingly well done this time around. The young cadet

James Stewart in STRATEGIC AIR COMMAND (1955).

was played by Anthony Newley, and a friend of his by Leslie Phillips.

John Gilling's direction gave the film a firmly convincing atmosphere and the audience was offered moments of great excitement and marvelous flying scenes. In the language of the critics: "The film was probably one of the most well-balanced and finely human portrayals of military life that has ever been made."

The aircraft used in the film were training planes and fighters like the Percival Provost and Hawker Hunter. The latter certainly is one of the most beautiful jet fighters ever built— the Spitfire of the jet age.

In 1957 a film was made about the life of Charles Lindbergh—the most famous flyer of them all. Its title was *THE SPIRIT OF ST. LOUIS* and unfortunately it was a bad film. Unaccountably, Billy Wilder, that veteran comedy director, was pressed into service as the director! Despite James Stewart's physical likeness to Lindbergh, Wilder failed to come to grips with the production. The best sequences in the film were from the pioneer days of flying circuses and mail planes. These segments were dramatic and humorous. But otherwise . . .

Next, air circuses. William Faulkner wrote a book entitled *Pylon* about the barnstorming time and also the many air races of the thirties. This book formed the basis for Universal's *TARNISHED ANGELS* (1957). It was directed by Douglas Sirk and appearing in the cast were Robert Stack, Rock Hudson and Dorothy Malone. It represented a dramatic description of the pioneer years of flying and the hectic development that took place during this epoch. It was a promising idea—but unfortunately thin soup made from good stock.

I will round off this section on slightly odd films with a few words about two efforts by veteran American directors: one by John Ford and the other by William Wellman. In 1957 Ford directed Metro's production of *THE WINGS OF EAGLES.*

Gary Cooper and Ralph Bellamy (standing) in THE COURT MARTIAL OF BILLY MITCHELL (1955).

Lower left: Ray Milland and Anthony Newley in HIGH FLIGHT (1957).

Right: Anthony Newley is rescued from his burning Hawker Hunter in HIGH FLIGHT (1957).

James Stewart as Charles Lindbergh in THE SPIRIT OF ST. LOUIS (1957).

Jack Hawkins in the British THE MAN IN THE SKY (1957).

Ray Milland in HIGH FLIGHT (1957).

Top left: James Stewart and Murray Hamilton have a talk in THE SPIRIT OF ST. LOUIS (1957).

Center: Dorothy Malone has something important to say to Robert Stack in THE TARNISHED ANGELS (1957).

Bottom: A very bad end! From Wellman's last motion picture— LAFAYETTE ESCADRILLE (1958).

It was a story about a well-known officer in the U.S. Navy—Commander Frank "Spig" Wead. For many years he had written original stories for the filmmakers of Hollywood, not just about flying but other subjects as well. Wead was above all a flyer, and also a good friend of Ford's. Unfortunately in this biography of his friend "Spig," Ford allowed his heart to speak rather than his head. The first half of the film is best ignored. The second half is acceptable, however. Here the director allows the U.S. Navy to fill the screen with all its aircraft carriers and airplanes as it proceeds to win the war in the Pacific. John Wayne played "Spig" Wead, with his usual single expression, and Wead's wife was played by the lovely Maureen O'Hara. Three splendid subordinate roles were played by Dan Dailey, Ward Bond and Ken Curtis.

And now let us end this chapter with Wellman's *LAFAYETTE ESCADRILLE* (1958).

Alas, this film did not merely represent the end of a chapter for this remarkable director—one of the most colorful personalities who ever lasted in Hollywood.

The original title of this production was to be *C'EST LA GUERRE,* and once again it was about the Lafayette Air Corps—volunteer pilots from the United States who flew for France during the First World War—which provided the background for many of the films we dealt with earlier. Wellman himself had flown in this fighter wing and was deeply involved personally and wished to do "something nice" with the story. But the wise men of the film company had other ideas. Jack Warner himself changed both the title and the content—Wellman was enraged and left the company for good. He never made another film. (In a separate chapter at the end of the book the reader can learn a little more about Mr. Wellman, who died in 1975.)

However, *LAFAYETTE ESCADRILLE* did bring about a new awakening of interest in the air battles of World War I. During the next ten to twelve years there would be a number of films dealing with this subject matter, and some of them were rather good.

Maureen O'Hara and John Wayne in John Ford's THE WINGS OF EAGLES (1957).

7001

A Time for Heroes

The space age had begun. Man had moved toward the conquest of the mysterious cosmos. In the autumn of 1956 American scientists, led by Werner von Braun, succeeded in firing a Redstone rocket 4,800 kilometers out into the Pacific Ocean. Three of the rocket's stage sections were equipped with solid fuel, the fourth section was empty. If this too had been filled with fuel they would have been able to place the rocket in orbit around the earth.

The Soviet Union succeeded in doing this the following year—1957. They fired a satellite into space, the name of which, *Sputnik,* immediately became famous throughout the world. A few years later (1961), the Russians succeeded in putting a man into space too. Encased in a small sphere-like vehicle, Major Yuri Gagarin circled the globe three times and became the first cosmonaut.

The United States had already begun its space program which was believed to be well advanced, but they now slipped behind the Russians. Despite the loss of prestige, the Americans took things in their stride and not until after they had made a couple of "test shots" from Cape Canaveral in Florida did they allow Lieutenant-Colonel John Glenn and Commander Scott Carpenter to repeat Gagarin's flight. In February and May 1962, the two men circled the globe three times each.

A S.E. 5 on patrol mission in Blake Edwards' DARLING LILI (1970).

The great development in space research would come during the 1960s. The X-15 airplane and the tremendously powerful giant rockets rapidly turned the course of scientists toward their primary goal—the moon.

During this exciting period of development in science and space travel, films too entered a new age. For a long time now the cinema had fought a losing battle against the rapid expansion of the television. Now, film was regaining some of its lost terrain with vast color spectacles in Cinerama and musicals such as *My Fair Lady* (1964), *The Sound of Music* (1965) and *Camelot* (1967). And in the repertoire of adventure there came such fine entries as *The Guns of Navarone* and *Lawrence of Arabia,* in 1961 and 1962, respectively.

A couple of ingenious producers, Albert R. Broccoli and Harry Saltzman, invested in an author by the name of Ian Fleming. The outcome: Superman and Tarzan both rolled into one character—James 007 Bond, licensed to kill. During this "pop age" decade, few films about flying saw the light of day. Of these few, however, there are one or two worth remembering.

England produced a relatively peaceful tale in 1960 called *CONE OF SILENCE,* with a cast that included Michael Craig, Bernard Lee and Peter Cushing. Charles Frend directed this film which told of a young pilot

(Craig) who was able to show that faulty construction was the cause of a disastrous passenger plane crash. In the crash the pilot (Lee) was killed; he also happened to be the father of the young hero's girlfriend. It was technically interesting and a film in which the audience could see how the investigation into the reasons for the crash was carried out.

An American writer by the name of John Hersey wrote a best seller—*The War Lover*—which Columbia found appealing enough to make a film of it. They appointed Philip Leacock as director and thus, in 1962, the movie public was presented with another film about Flying Fortresses and pilots involved in the bombing excesses over Europe in World War II.

Logically enough, the film was entitled *THE WAR LOVER* and the main roles were taken by Steve McQueen, Robert Wagner, and Shirley Ann Field. It was an engaging psychological drama about a bomber pilot (McQueen) with a charmed life. However, beneath his outward daring and fearlessness is a lonely man. He tries to protect himself by trusting in "luck." His inner insecurity causes him to waver on the border between hero and psychopath. He loves flying and his aircraft, which he regards as just as invulnerable as he himself is. His crew, too, begin to believe in his luck and imagine that their "Fortress" can fly undamaged through hellfire.

But luck changes. During a raid, the aircraft is severely shot up and some members of the crew are killed. Despite his own injuries and the dangerous damage to the plane, the pilot thinks he can fly her safely home. When they are over the English Channel two engines are out and a third is showing signs of packing up. They begin to lose altitude

Facing page: Steve McQueen as the insolent and daring—but lonesome—bomber pilot in THE WAR LOVER *from 1962, based on John Hersey's best-selling novel.*

Below left: Bernard Lee (right) and William Abney in "their last seconds . . ." from CONE OF SILENCE (1960).

Robert Wagner (left) and Steve McQueen in the WWII drama—THE WAR LOVER (1962).

rapidly and the second pilot (Wagner) tries to make his superior officer realize that it is all over and time to abandon the ship. Finally he gives in and orders the crew to jump. They parachute out and are afterwards picked up by an R.A.F. rescue boat. But the captain refuses to leave his machine. In a last attempt to show that his luck never gives out he tries to fly his aircraft up over the white cliffs of Dover, a maneuver that is doomed to failure and ends in disaster.

This was the end of the film. In the book he belly-lands in the sea and, as his comrades are being plucked out of the water, he clings fast to one of the propellers and follows his plane to the bottom. Actually this was the only deviation from the original story and the film otherwise adhered very closely to the book. Steve McQueen gave a convincing performance as the tragically fated pilot and *THE WAR LOVER* must unreservedly be ranked as an exceptional film about flying.

On the other hand, *A GATHERING OF EAGLES* must be regarded as only average. It was released in 1962 by Universal and was directed by Delbert Mann. Interesting technically, it was an oversimple story within the framework of crew training for the giant Boeing B-52 Stratofortress. There was some good aerial photography but a wooden performance by Rock Hudson. Others in the cast were Rod Taylor, Barry Sullivan and Mary Peach.

FLIGHT FROM ASHIYA (1964) showed how the American Air Rescue Service operated in the vast oceanic areas in the China Sea and around Japan. United Artists and Michael Anderson had Richard Widmark play a tough skipper on board a Grumman SA-16 Albatross. The dramatic high point in the film comes when Widmark, with George Chakiris as second pilot, tries to rescue some people in a lifeboat. It is blowing a full storm and, after letting Yul Brynner parachute down to the lifeboat, Widmark lands his plane in the raging sea. Just before he lands, he witnesses the crash of an accompanying aircraft. It was a rather exciting and technically well-made film, based on a novel by Elliot Arnold.

Rock Hudson in A GATHERING OF EAGLES (1962).

Yul Brynner as an air rescuer in the sea and air drama FLIGHT FROM ASHIYA (1964).

It appeared generally to be fashionable at the time to make films based on novels. *FATE IS THE HUNTER* (1964) was produced by Fox and was based on Ernest K. Gann's book of the same name. Unfortunately the film utilized only a fragment of Gann's minor masterpiece of autobiography, with disastrous results. Under Ralph Nelson's direction, it became only an anti-flying film. It almost scared the life out of would-be air passengers.

Glenn Ford plays a pilot and manager of an airline. He tries to discover if his old war buddy (Rod Taylor) has, through carelessness, been responsible for an air crash in which fifty-three people have been killed. Aside from a few exciting flying sequences and the drama between Ford and Taylor, this film had little to offer. The female leads were played by Nancy Kwan and Suzanne Pleshette.

633 SQUADRON was a film about a Mosquito squadron bombing a German rocket base located in a Norwegian fiord. Produced in 1964 by United Artists, this film was also based on a novel—by Frederick E. Smith.

The disaster is a big event. Television cameras and reporters are already on the location beside the burning wreckage. From FATE IS THE HUNTER (1964) *based on a novel by Ernest K. Gann.*

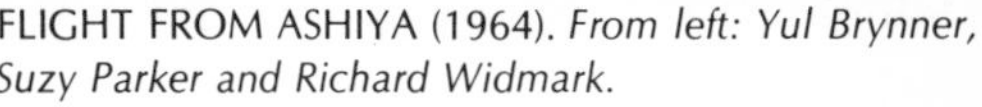

FLIGHT FROM ASHIYA (1964). *From left: Yul Brynner, Suzy Parker and Richard Widmark.*

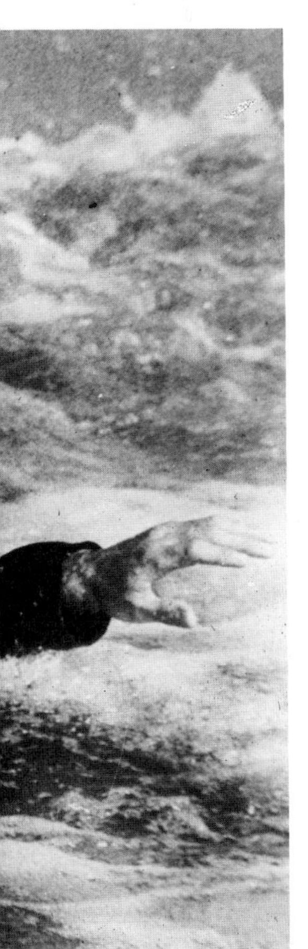

The leading roles in this well-made and rather exciting flying adventure were played by Cliff Robertson, George Chakiris and Maria Perschy. It was directed by Walter E. Grauman.

One of the most amusing films of the sixties was released in 1965. It was about the early years of aviation and was called *THOSE MAGNIFICENT MEN IN THEIR FLYING MACHINES*. It was made by Fox and directed by Ken Annakin, who, with the help of Ron Goodwin's appropriate music, succeeded in mixing together—if not a masterpiece—a couple of hours of very pleasing entertainment. The film is built around an air race sponsored by a large London newspaper. The year is 1909 and the point of the competition is to be the first to land in Paris in a London/Paris race. The prize, a large sum of money, attracts pilots from near and far.

There are many ups and downs before the prize is handed out and kisses are awarded. Gert Fröbe is unforgettable as a German officer in a Prussian helmet—chosen by the Kaiser himself to compete and win the race. —all for the honor of the Fatherland. The fact that he has never even seen an airplane before, other than in pictures, let alone flown one, is an irrelevant detail to a German officer, and to Gert Fröbe. It was very easy to laugh at this obstinate plump man as he held an instruction book in one hand and the joystick in the other while attempting to learn the mysteries of flying, and when he finally took to the air and drifted out over the narrow and very wet waters of the English Channel.

Terry Thomas, the always perfect and slightly mad Englishman, also inspired the flow of tears among the audience—but not tears of sadness. As the "bad boy" among the competitors, he represented a constant threat to the others by regularly sabotaging their machines. However, his efforts frequently turned out to be pitfalls into which he himself fell, to the unconcealed pleasure of the spectators.

There was a whole gallery of stars appearing in this film: Stuart Whitman, James Fox, Sarah Miles, Robert Morley, Jean-Pierre Cassel and Alberto Sordi, and as special guest artist, Red Skelton.

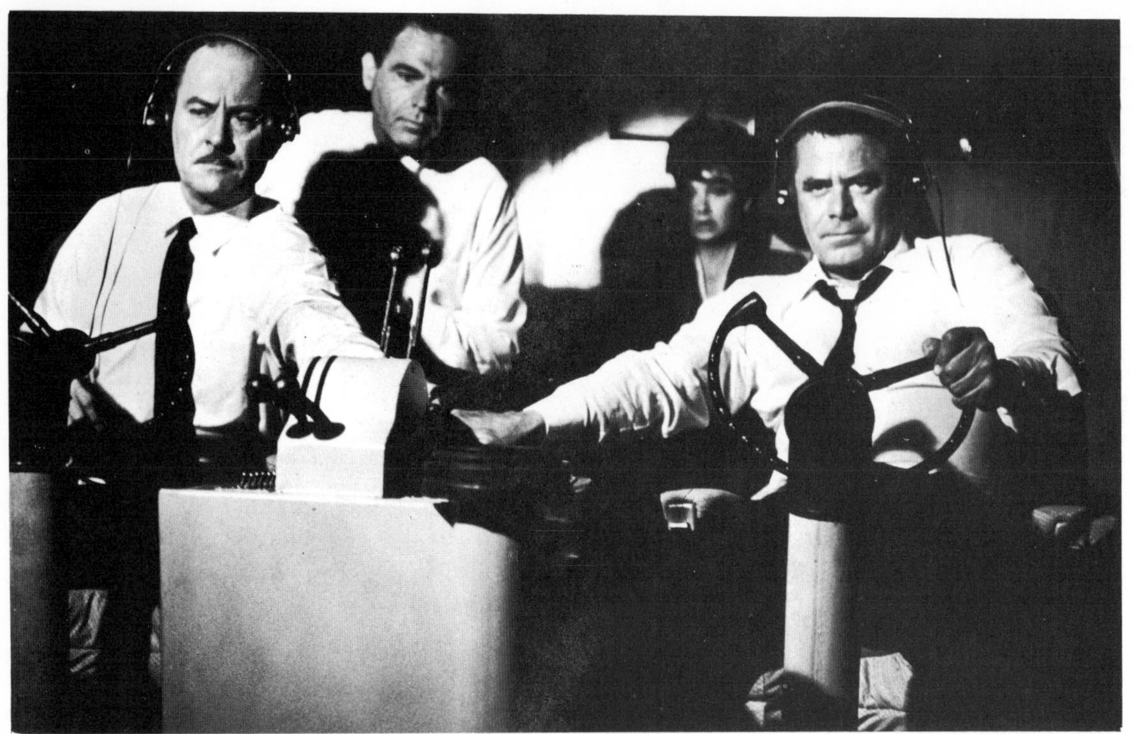

Glenn Ford fights the controls in Ralph Nelson's FATE IS THE HUNTER *(1964). Behind, a glimpse of Suzanne Pleshette and Nehemiah Persoff. The copilot (left) is unknown.*

Flying machines used in the movie included precise replicas of such rare beauties as the Santos-Dumont Demoiselle and Levavasseur Antoinette. There were also genuine ancient "flying string bags" of the Avro and Curtiss type in this very amusing film.

Fox was also responsible for the next flight drama, in which Robert Aldrich boldly went into the desert to achieve the right tension for *THE FLIGHT OF THE PHOENIX*. It was made in 1965 and had James Stewart in the role of a veteran transport pilot who crash-lands his Fairchild C-119 Packet, loaded with passengers, in the middle of the Sahara Desert. Among the passengers who survive there is an engineer (Hardy Krüger) who has

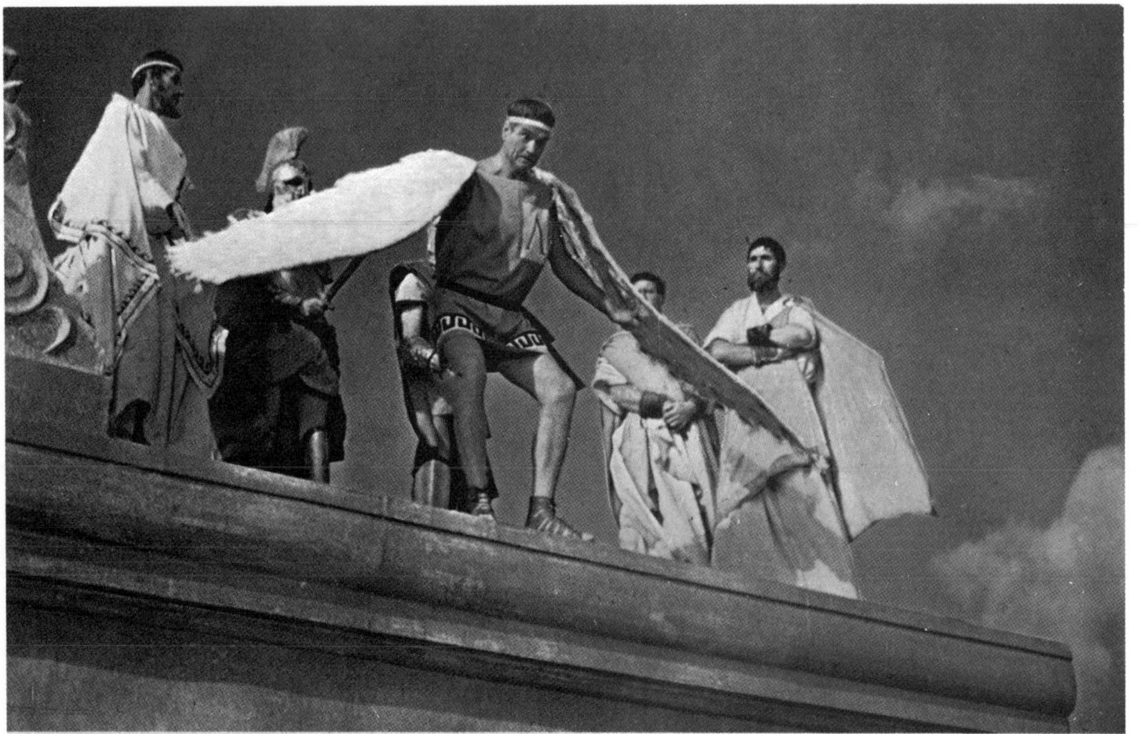

A divine "Icarus," personified by Red Skelton, preparing to try his wings in the very entertaining Fox spectacle from 1965— THOSE MAGNIFICENT MEN IN THEIR FLYING MACHINES.

British comic actor
Thomas can here
en after a more or
successful landing
in THOSE
AGNIFICENT MEN
IN THEIR FLYING
MACHINES (1965).

worked on the building of aircraft. With the help of Stewart and the others, he builds a new plane from the wreckage of the old one. With this machine they hope to fly back to civilization. In this they succeed, but not without much sweat and tears.

In fact, a "real" airplane was built for this rather dramatic film from parts salvaged from a genuine C-119. It was constructed in accordance with the plans contained in a book by Elleston Trevor upon which the film adventure was based. The well-known stunt pilot Paul Mantz flew the plane. Sadly he was killed when the aircraft broke in two and crashed during the film work. In honor of Mantz this particular dramatic scene was kept in the film. Paul Mantz, who had flown since he was fifteen or sixteen years old, was one of the best known stunt pilots in Hollywood. Together with his friend Frank Tallman, he formed a company that worked exclusively on the making of films—Tallmantz Aviation. They worked out of the Orange County Airport (now called John Wayne Airport) south of Los Angeles where they established a museum called The Movieland of the Air. After Mantz's death, Tallman took over as managing director of the company until 1978 when he was killed in a crash during a reconnaissance flight in the mountains.

From 1965 the adventure of flying entered a period of real nostalgic flashbacks to the great wars of 1914–18 and 1939–45.

633 SQUADRON (1964).

Facing page, top: How will they get the rebuilt machine up into the air? From THE FLIGHT OF THE PHOENIX (1965).

Center: THE BLUE MAX (1966). *Near the camera a Fokker Triplane and behind it Fokker D VIIs.*

Bottom: Another briefing—this time it is Christopher George who shows his men what's next on the schedule. From THE 1,000 PLANE RAID (1969).

From left: Richard Attenborough, James Stewart and Hardy Kruger in Robert Aldrich's air and desert drama THE FLIGHT OF THE PHOENIX *from 1965.*

There were a number of productions in which we were able to see how heroes flying over the trenches of Verdun won or lost the First World War. We were also able to see how "the Few" stopped Hitler in 1940 from taking over little England. We could see how the great armadas of bombers systematically pounded the German war machine in the madness of World War II.

In 1966, Fox and John Guillermin gave us a filmed version of a book about the 1914–18 war. This was *THE BLUE MAX* which showed us for once the German side of the conflict and centered on a character who might be described as an anti-hero.

The story—taken from Jack D. Hunter's book of the same title—is about a young German Army officer who becomes a fighter pilot after realizing that the muddy existence of trench warfare does not suit his personal-

From left: Cliff Robertson, Maria Perschy and George Chakiris in 633 SQUADRON (1964).

ity. At the time the German air corps was populated largely by aristocrats, and our young hero has some difficulties adjusting since his comrades regard him as a social climber. In order to show them that he is as good as they are he makes up his mind to become the best pilot there is—to win the highest medal the Kaiser awards, *Pour le Mérite,* popularly known as The Blue Max. He lets nothing stand in his way of achieving this goal. He is a very good pilot and rapidly shoots down sufficient numbers of enemy planes to be classed as an "ace." But he is also cold, extremely arrogant and completely ruthless. If necessary he will walk over the bodies of his comrades to gain his goal.

Finally he reaches it. He has become one of the best pilots in Germany and wears the light-blue ribbon of the *Pour le Mérite* around his neck. But even the best can make an error or have bad luck. He meets his fate during the test flight of a new fighter.

Aside from its highly realistic atmosphere and well-developed characters, the film was not up to expectations. George Peppard was completely miscast as the unscrupulous antihero, and his brief love affair with the beautiful countess (Ursula Andress) was rather wet. It was evidently only included in order to display the charms of this beautiful actress—with and without clothes. On the other hand, there were a number of good performances by Jeremy Kemp as an aristocratic pilot, James Mason as the general, and Karl Michael Vogler's interpretation of the chivalrous but misled squadron leader.

The flying scenes in *THE BLUE MAX* were photographed by Skeets Kelly and his staff and were exciting and excellently shot. Among other things, there was a thrilling dogfight between an Albatros D III and an S.E. 5 at very low altitude. These flying scenes were directed by Tony Squire and constituted the only real quality in the film.

In 1969 a film was produced that tried to show straightforwardly how a "thousand-plane raid" was planned and executed against German industries. It was entitled *THE 1,000 PLANE RAID* and was released by United Artists and directed by Boris Sa-

George Peppard is here awarded "his" Pour Le Mérite in John Guillermin's THE BLUE MAX (1966).

BLUE MAX

20th CENTURY-FOX GEORGE PEPPARD · JAMES MASON · URSULA ANDRESS

i "THE BLUE MAX" JEREMY KEMP · KARL MICHAEL VOGLER · ANTON DIFFRING

PROD: CHRISTIAN FERRY EX. PROD: ELMO WILLIAMS REGI: JOHN GUILLERMIN

FÖR FILMEN AV: BEN BARZMAN och BASILIO FRANCHINA SCENARIO: DAVID PURSALL och JACK SEDDON och GERALD HANLEY CINEMASCOPE FÄRG: DeLUX

gal. The flying sequences and battle scenes were largely "canned material" pressed into the framework of a simple story starring Christopher George, Laraine Stephens and J. D. Cannon.

In 1969 came the film that all flying enthusiasts and people interested in movies thought could be "the flying film to end all flying films": *BATTLE OF BRITAIN,* which was released by United Artists under the direction of Guy Hamilton.

The two producers Broccoli and Saltzman, who had been making a mint for years out of the James Bond films, considered how they could best make use of all their money. Saltzman decided to invest in a spectacle that would immortalize all those who had fought for England in the R.A.F. during the dramatic autumn months of 1940.

No expense was spared to create as authentic a background as possible. Old Spitfires and Hurricanes were tracked down and restored, many of them still in flying condition. In some cases, the producers had found different versions of these aircraft, but skillful technicians were able to convert these into the appropriate types and no one can see the difference in the finished film.

The Spanish Air Force contributed the aircraft for the German side by lending a whole wing of Heinkel He 111s and a squadron of Messerschmitt Me 109s. Both types of Spanish Air Force planes were equipped with Hispano engines and so were slightly different from the original aircraft. But what are a few minor details? It was to be the greatest adventure story about flying ever made!

Sadly, this was not to be the case. Certainly it was enjoyable to see all these fine old aircraft in the air again, but something was missing. A theme. A real story that told more about the people involved. There was no such story even though the writer of the screenplay supplied some instructions as to how Hamilton should use his large corps of actors.

Basically, the redeeming features of the film consisted of dramatic film material in the dogfight montage and a segment containing rapid and vivid scenes of the battle's final stage. There was no dialogue in these

All stills on these two pages are from THE BATTLE OF BRITAIN (1969). *Top left: Robert Shaw as Squadron Leader "Skipper." Center left: A pair of Hurricanes belonging to the Polish squadron. Lower left: The German fighter boss—Major Falke—played by Mannfred Reddenmann. This character was based on a real German fighter ace—Adolf Galland. On this page: Spitfires attack German Heinkel He 111s escorted by Messerschmitts.*

sequences except for the occasional radio voice coming through the action and the very effective musical score—"Battle of the Air," composed by Sir William Walton. The music envisions the dramatic, rapid progress of the battle, the swirling aircraft, and the spirit of victory of the pilots and their fearful courage. There was excitement here, a sense of commitment—for a few brief minutes.

The rest of the music for the film was composed by Ron Goodwin. There were two main themes—"Battle of Britain Theme" and "Ace High March"—which struck the right tone in the shifts between the events on the British side and those on the German side.

There were many well-known names among the staff of actors: Sir Laurence Olivier as Air Marshal Sir Hugh Dowding (Commander of the British Fighter Command), and R.A.F. pilots played by Trevor Howard, Kenneth More, Robert Shaw, Michael Caine, Christopher Plummer, Edward Fox and Ian McShane along with many others. Susannah York appeared in the film as an officer in the WAAF. On the German side, Hermann Goering was played by cabaret artist Hein Reiss, and fighter ace Major Falke by Manfred Reddenmann (a character based on General Adolf Galland, head of the Luftwaffe Fighter Command).

Concluding remarks: *BATTLE OF BRITAIN* had many people and aircraft and a great deal of Saltzman's money, lots of advanced special effects—and almost nothing of any human interest.

The following year (1970), United Artists released *MOSQUITO SQUADRON,* directed by Boris Sagal and with David McCallum, Suzanne Neve and David Buck. It was a very weak story about bomb attacks on German rocket bases.

"When Mata Hari met Biggles" would have been a suitable title for the production that Blake Edwards directed for Paramount in 1970. The real title was *DARLING LILI,* and once again we were back in the First World War. Julie Andrews performed as a much-wooed entertainer who did a little extra work on the side as a spy for the Germans. Rock Hudson played the young Allied flyer who lands in her net between his tussles with Richthofen and *his* buddies.

David McCallum in MOSQUITO SQUADRON (1970).

Here is a quote from a review: "Hudson displays a skill in the flying sequences that is not inferior to the boy-hero Biggles. Once, when he is forced to land in enemy territory, he simply steals the Red Baron's own plane for the return journey. He is, however, less successful in the battle against Mata Hari's double, Julie Andrews. He passes on so much important information that the fall of Germany seems unlikely."

Blake Edwards did not really do a bad job, but it is the technical aspects that one remembers; the actual substance of the film is thin indeed. Jeremy Kemp was among the more memorable actors; so too was Lance Percival, very amusing as a flight lieutenant

De Havilland Mosquitos taxiing out for takeoff in MOSQUITO SQUADRON (1970).

Rock Hudson and Lance Comfort in high adventures. From Blake Edwards' DARLING LILI (1970).

who filled himself with whisky to gain courage.

In 1970 Paramount also released a highly unusual film called *CATCH 22*. It was based on Joseph Heller's best-selling novel of the same name and was about a bomber squadron in Sicily. Mike Nichols was responsible for this film and the action in it followed Heller's book closely.

The content is absurd, very funny and very serious. The plot is somewhat complicated which makes it rather difficult to summarize. The main theme, however, is basically this: if you wish to do something—take leave, be admitted to the hospital, stop flying, or, more than anything else, go home—then just ask the advice of your superior officer. He will always say NO! Always refer to the clause of military protocol called "Catch 22."

The character who constantly strives to persuade his superiors is a bombardier, Yossarian. He has completed his twenty-five tours and wants to return home—HOME! He is now up to fifty-seven tours simply because it says in Catch 22 that once you have completed the latest series of tours you are required to do an additional ten more. A formulation which means that when you have completed fifty tours you must do an additional ten, and so on and on. . . .

Everything in the film is based upon the mad pointlessness of this assumption, which does not mean that the film is a farce—on the contrary! It is very funny—obviously—but it is also gruesome, realistic in a serious sense and giving a convincing portrait of the fundamental insanity of war, military madness and bureaucracy.

Alan Arkin gave a wonderful performance as Yossarian and Martin Balsam played his more or less mad chief. Orson Welles's vast figure was used to inflate the uniform of a general on inspection. And Anthony Perkins walked through the whole film as a weakling dressed in priest's garb, with his hands clasped in front of him: he was the wing's chaplain. On *Dumbo,* the aircraft that Yossarian served in, Art Garfunkel was the second pilot.

A large number of B-25 Mitchell bombers were required in the filming of *CATCH 22*. Stunt pilot Frank Tallman was approached

From Mike Nichols' CATCH 22 (1970) we can see in the cockpit: the copilot (Arthur Garfunkel) and in the nose of Dumbo a glimpse of Alan Arkin (as Yossarian).

Facing page: Yossarian's unit of B-25 Mitchells are cleared for takeoff to carry out their next tour—all according to "Catch 22."

and he succeeded in scraping together twenty or so of these relics from World War II—best known from "the thirty seconds over Tokyo."

Tallman took these planes, with machine guns, bombs and reserve parts, to a God-forsaken place in Mexico where the terrain was similar to that in Sicily. He remained there with his "wing" for four months, until the film was completed. But it was worth it. There are not many flying sequences in *CATCH 22* nor are they long, but they are all first class.

Pearl Harbor, the American naval base on Hawaii which was the center of many exciting events in many films, also supplied the background for a film released by Fox in 1970. It was entitled *TORA! TORA! TORA!* and was the true story of what happened when the invincible United States was caught napping by the Imperial Japanese Navy and Air Force.

If *BATTLE OF BRITAIN* was something of a disappointment, then this latter film was really a pleasant surprise—at least in the eyes of this author. The story is told, bit by bit and perhaps a little too detailed, of how the Japanese Navy and its Air Force plan and execute the attack on the American base. It also shows to some extent what happened on the American side and how many small errors committed by a variety of people combined to create chaos and discord—a tragedy of errors that found everyone lying comfortably asleep when the surprise attack began on the morning of December 7, 1941.

One of the subtleties of the filming of this most interesting phase of the war was that both sides were allowed to speak their respective languages. In other words, when Admiral Yamamoto discussed the situation with his admirals, he spoke Japanese. English was spoken in the American staff headquarters. This added considerable authenticity to the events. A great deal of effort also went into converting various types of suitable aircraft into likenesses of the original planes that carried out the attack. This was also true of the American aircraft.

Richard Fleischer, who directed it in cooperation with the Japanese, managed to hold all the strings together fairly well and thus provided some moments of technically

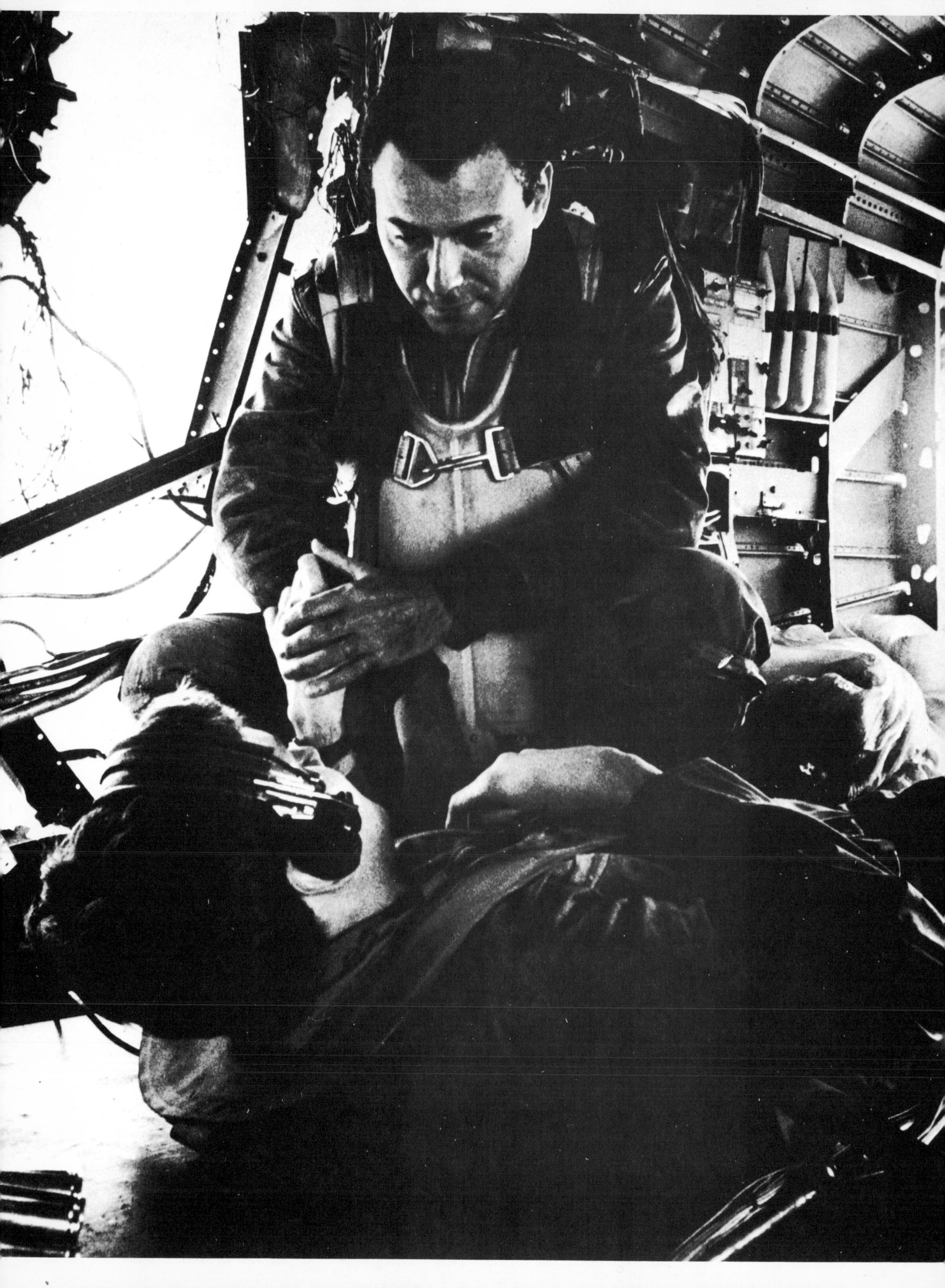

Alan Arkin as Bombardier Yossarian in CATCH 22 (1970).

The strafing on Hickam Field at Pearl Harbor has taken place. From TORA! TORA! TORA! (1970).

Below, left: The last part of the approach. It's early in the morning of December 7, 1941. From TORA! TORA! TORA! (1970).

Lieutenant Colonel Mitsuo Fuchida (Takahiro Tamura), who led the infamous attack against the Navy base at Pearl Harbor in December 1941. "Tora!" is the Japanese word for "Tiger!" and the signal code for a successful mission.

brilliant historical flashback to what "actually happened." It was a very big cast and we will mention only a few of the names: Martin Balsam, Joseph Cotten, E.G. Marshall, Tatsuya Mihashi and Takahiro Tamura.

In 1971, United Artists decided once again to enchant the cinema audience with a production about the First World War. This was *VON RICHTHOFEN AND BROWN*, directed by Roger Corman. It attempted to tell the story of the legendary German fighter ace being shot down by the young Canadian pilot Roy Brown. In the history books, Brown is the one who is credited with the Red Baron's fall. No one knows for sure if it was bullets from his guns which really ended the German flyer's life, but it is generally thought to be the case.

This was not a bad film—in my opinion, better than *THE BLUE MAX*. John Phillip Law gave a convincing portrayal of the Red Baron and Don Stroud appeared as his victorious antagonist.

In 1973, 20th Century-Fox released a little story about an old pilot from the 1914–18 war. It was entitled *ACE ELI AND RODGER OF THE SKIES*—a fine little tale based on a story by Steven Spielberg. John Erman directed this film about the veteran fighter pilot Eli and the time when flying was still "young"

John Phillip Law shows his fighting face as the legendary "Red Baron" in VON RICHTHOFEN AND BROWN (1971).

and the world still relatively innocent—except for Eli's son Rodger—Rodger of the skies. Cliff Robertson played the part of Eli while his offspring Rodger, who harbored wild dreams of the future, was played by Eric Shea. The female lead was taken by Pamela Franklin.

A film that was shot at about the same time and concerned the same period as *ACE ELI AND RODGER OF THE SKIES* was Universal's *THE GREAT WALDO PEPPER* (1975). The time is 1926 and the place Nebraska, United States. Waldo is a young former fighter pilot with some brief experience of the air battles over the Western Front. In the true meaning of the word, he is "mad" about flying. After being demobilized he makes his living by taking up passengers and after a time he ends up in a flying circus. Most of his time is spent dreaming about meeting one of the great enemy aces. His brief period at the front was too short to enable him to engage in any dogfights—and certainly he had no chance to shoot down any enemy planes.

During a flying exhibition, Waldo crashes and is severely injured. Although he finally recovers, his future now looks very dark. In fact the newly established aviation authority has taken away his licence. When he recovers from his injuries he goes into a depression and becomes more or less an alcoholic.

Cliff Robertson and Eric Shea in the Fox film ACE ELI AND RODGER OF THE SKIES (1973). *The airplane is a Curtiss Jenny.*

Eventually, under an assumed name, he gets a job as a stunt pilot in Hollywood. At last his dream is fulfilled: in the shooting of a film, he is to portray a British fighter pilot who meets a German ace man-to-man in an air duel. The "enemy" pilot is a real German ex-ace by the name of Ernst Kessler (a character based on the German flyer Ernst Udet, who worked for a time after the armistice in the United States as an air acrobat and even as a Hollywood stunt pilot).

The exciting battle begins and the cameras roll, but then the whole scene develops a more serious twist than the two men had envisioned—suddenly they are back in the past, they are now real enemies and out to kill each other.

They very nearly do, but come to their senses at last and return to normal. In the final scenes, Waldo turns his aircraft upwards into the sun and the freedom that all flyers seek, beyond the sun-rimmed clouds up in the ice-blue skies.

The film was directed by George Roy Hill, whose original story idea it was, and the screenplay was written by William Goldman. Robert Redford played Waldo Pepper, which was not perhaps such a bad idea, except that his performance was robot-like. His acting was easily outdone by two Swedes appearing in the film: Bo Svenson, as Waldo's buddy Axel Olson, and Bo Brundin in a finely wrought portrayal of the German pilot Kessler. The flying scenes were beautiful, exciting, and occasionally amusing, in this film about young drifters who risked their lives in a mad pursuit of money and fame.

ACES HIGH, produced in 1976 by S. Benjamin Fisz and directed by Jack Gold, was a film about real heroes. It was based on a well-known play called *Journey's End* by R.C. Sheriff—and first filmed in the early thirties—and was concerned with what young flyers were really like in World War I. It also dealt with the age of these young

Barnstorming pilots flew like this—at the lowest imaginable altitude down a street somewhere in Nebraska. From THE GREAT WALDO PEPPER *(1975). This stunt was carried out by the legendary Hollywood stunt pilot Frank Tallman. The machine is a Curtiss Jenny.*

men (hardly more than schoolboys) and how frightened and unsure of themselves they actually were when they came eye to eye with a ruthless enemy, frequently only to meet a quick, violent death.

The story briefly is as follows: in the fall of 1917, young Stephen Croft (Peter Firth) arrives in France. He is sent to a fighter squadron, the chief of which is the great idol of his school days, John Gresham. Now Gresham is an alcoholic and less than enchanted at having the youngster in his squadron. This is partly because he simply does not want such young pilots and partly because he is attracted to Croft's beautiful sister. He is also afraid that certain unfavorable aspects of his behavior will come to light. However, the young would-be fighter pilot does not see any change in his idol, especially after Gresham has saved him from attacking enemy planes during his first mission.

Within a week the young man has rapidly become a pilot and has almost completely mastered his plane, but on the seventh day he collides with an enemy aircraft. However, he manages to crash-land safely and make his way back to base. Gresham, who believes him to be lost, strikes his name from the squadron rolls and then is overjoyed when he sees his young pupil come walking through the morning mist—tired, a little frightened but richer in experience.

In fact, it was mostly young men like Croft who survived—they did so because they were not ashamed to feel fear along with their will to fight and win, and to show their skill. Our young hero volunteers to go on a dangerous reconnaissance flight together with an older colleague. They are to take photographs over enemy lines before an impending offensive. The older man, who is not allowed to fly because of an earlier injury, has shown a warm personal interest in Croft and during this brief span of time they have become friends. They complete their mission and must fly through a gauntlet of heavy fire on their return. Happy at his success, Croft

Malcolm McDowell as Squadron Leader Gresham in ACES HIGH (1976).

ACES HIGH (1976). *From left: Peter Firth, Christopher Plummer and Malcolm McDowell.*

gets out of the plane. They made it! But in the aft cockpit the older man slumps dead with his camera on his knees. Only a couple of days later, Gresham strikes the name of the young pilot from the rolls again. His time at the front lasted exactly nine days.

Malcolm McDowell played the part of the experienced but still youthful squadron leader Gresham who, due to the hopelessness of his task, has taken to the bottle (compare *DAWN PATROL,* 1930 and '38). Croft's good friend and older colleague, Sinclair, was played by Christopher Plummer who showed in this film that he is a fine character actor. The scenes between him and Firth were quite remarkable. Simon Ward played one of Croft's other comrades. He was a terrified pilot who could never bring himself to join his comrades on patrol—a tragic portrait but with much underlying realism.

Karen Black as the tough air hostess Nancy Pryor in the air spectacle AIRPORT 75 (1975).

The flying scenes in *ACES HIGH* were very well done. There were a number of authentic aircraft in it as well as other old biplanes that were converted to look like S.E. 5s and Fokkers.

Since 1976 there have been no authentic films about flying. During the seventies there were a couple of catastrophe films about passenger planes, but only one of them was a legitimate flying film. This was *AIRPORT 75,* released by Universal in 1975 and with Charlton Heston and George Kennedy as the brave heroes.

It was about the collision between a Boeing 747 "jumbo jet" and a small private plane. The smaller plane crashes immediately but the jumbo jet remains in the air despite a large hole in the pilot's section. Both pilots are dead but the aircraft continues to fly on its auto-pilot. A cool and clever air hostess (Karen Black) manages to fly the plane manually—with the help of the automatic pilot and radio instructions from the ground. She has to do this while awaiting a rescue operation. This consists of using a fast helicopter to put Charlton Heston on board the plane. He will attempt to board the big jet through the hole in the cockpit. The whole operation seems insane, not to say impossible. But in fact it was done in the film using real aircraft and the only thing that was not authentic was the actual boarding of the plane through the hole. They could not very well cut up a real 747. But if they had, they would certainly have really put a man through the hole. In any case, it was very cleverly and expensively filmed over the Rocky Mountains, and some moments were really exciting although on the whole it was a rather watery stew.

In a few Cinerama films, such as *THIS IS CINERAMA* (1952) and *IT'S A MAD, MAD,*

MAD, MAD WORLD (1963), there were a number of really great flying sequences. In the latter, Mickey Rooney appeared as a slightly nutty pilot who makes a living by taking up passengers for fairly large sums of money. His airplane is virtually a wreck—an old Ford Trimotor that has seen much better days. There was one scene in the film that provoked a great deal of laughter.

In the same film, stunt pilot Frank Tallman flew a two-engine Beechcraft right through a gigantic billboard, a maneuver that could have ended badly. Tallman trained for a couple of weeks by flying through a billboard made of wooden ribs and canvas, but when the day for actually shooting the scene arrived, a real billboard stood in its place—that is to say, one made of heavy planks and plastic, mounted between two steel beams. The space between the beams and the wing tips was a meter on either side. Tallman made the approach and roared through the billboard at 250 km/h. Wood, sheet metal and glass flew in all directions and Tallman requested immediate permission to land at a nearby field, over his radio. He had lost one engine and the other one was functioning only by the grace of God. In addition, his windshield was completely gone. He landed the plane safely and, although the aircraft was badly damaged, Tallman climbed out uninjured. The photographers had taken many meters of film that were much more than merely acceptable.

Tallman also flew the same aircraft right through a hangar in another sequence in the

Facing page: Sterling Hayden as the crazy General Ripper and Peter Sellers as Captain Mandrake in the amusing but also gloomy DR. STRANGELOVE (1964). *Sellers played dual roles as Mandrake and Dr. Strangelove himself.*

The high point of AIRPORT 75 (1975): *the attempt to get a new pilot (Heston) on board the stricken jumbo from a fast helicopter. Well done and very exciting!*

PEACE IS OUR PROFESSION

*Henry Fonda as the President of the United States in the nuclear horror story—*FAIL SAFE (1964).

film. His problem here was that the height of the roof was not sufficient for him to do this trick with his landing gear down, which would have been safer since he could if need be "roll" the airplane along on its wheels if he flew too low. As we said, it was a very low ceiling! Tallman solved the problem by flying through the hangar at 250 km/h—with his landing gear up!

Two other films that contained really good flying sequences were the amusing, but frightening, *DR. STRANGELOVE* (1964) and the dramatic *FAIL SAFE* made the same year. Basically, they both dealt with the same subject—madmen who decide that they must press the button: the "ultimate" button! These madmen believe that the solution to all our problems lies in total hydrogen-bomb warfare. In the former, the main roles were played by Sterling Hayden and Peter Sellers, and very well played at that. In *FAIL SAFE,* the fate of the world rested in the hands of the American President, in this case Henry Fonda.

The *AIRPORT* series continued with *AIRPORT '80—THE CONCORDE.* The film starred the world's most controversial aircraft and featured Alain Delon, Susan Blakely, George Kennedy and Bibi Anderson. Unfortunately, this film must be included in

Actor Robert Duvall and a McDonnell F-4 Phantom in THE GREAT SANTINI (1979).

Alain Delon as an airline commander in the new "airport adventure" AIRPORT '80—THE CONCORDE (1979/80). *The plane behind him is the controversial, but famous, supersonic airliner Concorde.*

the collection of flops. Despite the serious subject matter, the film alternates between false drama and cheap farce.

The "catastrophe" genre was spoofed in the 1980 film *AIRPLANE!* (also titled *FLYING HIGH*). The youthful Hollywood trio of Jim Abrahams, David and Jerry Zucker achieved something approaching a comic masterpiece. Derived from the classic American "crazy" tradition, the film also shows the influences of *MAD* magazine and England's Monty Python group.

Robert Hay is the star, but appearances by veteran actors from the era of "heroic" flying films improve the hilarity. Robert Stack, Lloyd Bridges and Leslie Nielsen are part of this liberating belly laugh.

A fine film about modern American military officers was released in 1979 by Warner Brothers. *THE GREAT SANTINI* stars Robert Duvall as Colonel Bull Meechum, a Marine pilot of the old school. The film, also called *THE GIFT OF FURY*, was based on a novel by Pat Conroy. It was adapted and directed by Lewis John Carlino.

In this excellent psychological portrait of the man behind the facade of a fighter pilot, Duvall is recalled to active duty to command a troublesome squadron of fighter pilots. He fulfills the duty with honor, but the colonel is a tyrant at home, treating his family as raw recruits and driving his understanding wife (Blythe Danner) towards a mental breakdown. The eldest son (Michael O'Keefe) is cruelly kept in check by the father and is expected to be best at everything and a real "man's man."

The son's best friend, a black boy, is attacked by a gang of white hoodlums. The son defies his father and rushes to help his friend, but is too late, and the boy dies.

Colonel Meechum realizes his ideas about a military upbringing have gone too far. A

THE PILOT (1980)

warmer and more honest relationship develops between them, and the whole family starts a new life. But, again, it is too late. During a routine night flight, the colonel crashes and is killed.

On the technical side, *THE GREAT SANTINI* has some beautiful flying scenes with the powerful McDonnell F-4 Phantom jet.

Another American flying drama is *THE PILOT* (1980). Cliff Robertson directed this film and also played the leading role of Mike Hagen, an airline pilot. The controversial story deals with the problem of alcohol.

Captain Hagen is well aware of his own drinking problem, but won't concede that, for professional reasons, he should take time off until he is well again. Flying is as important a stimulant to Hagen as alcohol, and the pilot succeeds, at first, in juggling his drinking and flying timetables. While trying to rehabilitate himself, his big DC-8 crashes on takeoff. The bloody irony is that Hagen is not responsible. A watchdog pilot assigned to keep an eye on Hagen causes the crash.

Robertson gives fine directing and acting performances in *THE PILOT*. Others appearing in the film were Dana Andrews, Horst Buchholz and Gordon Macrae. Macrae's last film was *The Best Things in Life are Free* in 1956.

During the past few years there have been a number of television series and movies about flying.

A co-production from Australia and New Zealand, *SOLO* (1978) focused on the life of a flying fire ranger. The ranger, played by Vincent Gil, makes daily flights over the vast forests of the New Zealand wilderness. His best friend is another "hermit" who lives seven months of the year in a fire control tower. Their world is disrupted by the arrival of a pretty young girl (Lisa Peers). The story line is not excessively original, but the real enjoyment of the film consists in a number of flights in an old Tiger Moth. John Blick was the director.

Notable for a certain romantic realism was *USA: THE WINDS OF KITTY HAWK* made in 1979–80. The feature-length, semi-documentary describes how the famous Wilbur and Orville Wright struggled to achieve the first flight in a self-powered heavier-than-

From the different science fiction story, CLOSE ENCOUNTERS OF THE THIRD KIND (1977).

Actor Keir Dullea in 2001: A SPACE ODYSSEY (1969).

air machine. The retelling of this historically important event is both technically and dramatically convincing. The Wright brothers were portrayed by Michael Moriarty (Wilbur) and David Huffman (Orville). E. W. Swackhammer was the director.

Television series which feature flying have sometimes been inspired by feature films. This was the case with *TWELVE O'CLOCK HIGH.* It was based on the 1949 film in which Gregory Peck had the leading role as General Savage. Robert Lansing won the role in the TV version, which aired from 1964 to 1967 in the United States and has been seen often in syndication.

The legendary Marine Corps pilot Gregory "Pappy" Boyington has been the topic of the TV series *BLACK SHEEP SQUADRON.* Boyington is played by actor Robert Conrad. Pappy fought with the Marines in the Pacific during the Second World War and became a flying ace in the Vought F4U Corsair. During 1941–42 he was a member of the "Flying Tigers." He shot down his 28th enemy aircraft in January 1944, but was then shot down himself and crashed at sea. Boyington was rescued by a Japanese submarine and was held as a prisoner of war until the surrender in 1945. Word of his capture had not been communicated to American authorities.

An American comic strip was the basis for a television series in the 1950s. Milton Caniff's *STEVE CANYON* was the core of a half-hour adventure series that also served as good propaganda for the Air Force. Lieutenant Colonel Steve Canyon was played by Dean Fredericks; Jerry Paris was the commanding officer.

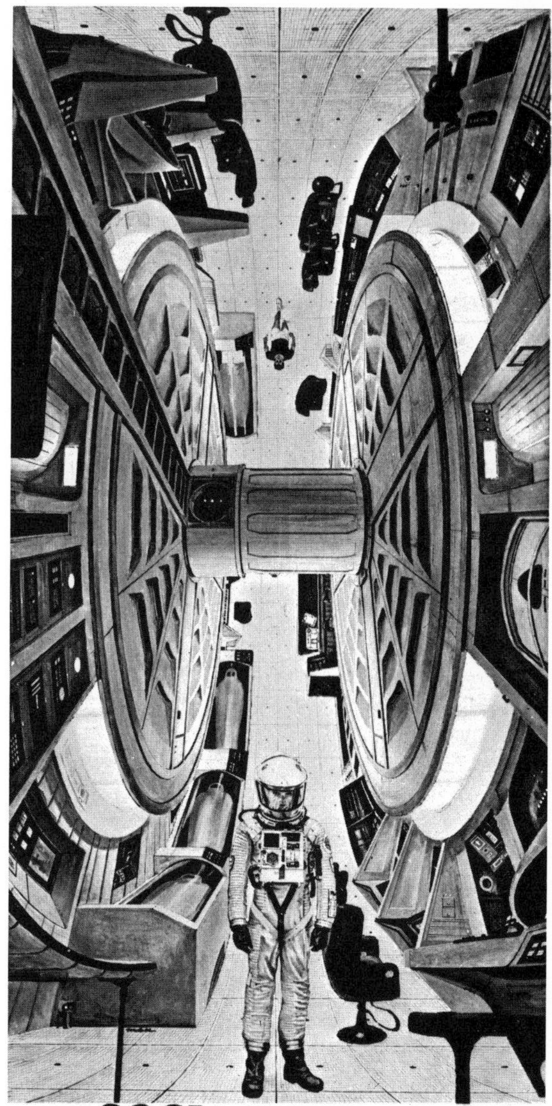

During the sixties, the British produced a television series about flying. *THE PATHFINDERS* told the stories of pilots who flew in advance of bomber squadrons to mark the targets with colored incendiary bombs. Casualties were extremely high in this group until the advent of the highly maneuverable Mosquito. The series lead was played by Scottish actor Robert Urquhart.

At the end of the decade and on into the eighties, space adventures began to predominate, with all the action relegated to the cosmos.

Stanley Kubrick's fantastic creation, *2001—A SPACE ODYSSEY* (1968), lighted the way for new generations, showed the way to the future. With productions such as *STAR WARS* and *CLOSE ENCOUNTERS OF THE THIRD KIND* (both 1977), film producers, directors and technicians showed that outer space with its millions of galaxies will be the target of cameras during the final two decades of this century—to the year 2000 A.D.

A typical example of the genre was *FLASH GORDON*. Pre-release publicity promised a film that would make the colossals—*STAR WARS, THE EMPIRE STRIKES BACK, BATTLESTAR GALACTICA AND STAR TREK*—seem amateur by comparison. Unfortunately, the Dino de Laurentiis production was disappointing.

The charm that characterized Alex Raymond's classic series, and even to some extent the Buster Crabbe serial of the thirties, was lost in the mammoth production. The story line and characters were smothered in a flood of technical chicanery.

However, the performances of some in the cast rose above this: Max von Sydow as the classic villain Mong, and Topal in the role of Doctor Zarkow. Sam Jones, who played Flash, certainly looked the part; if it is possible for a person to be a look-alike of a comic strip character. But this alone was not sufficient to make a convincing figure of the No. 1 space hero.

STAR WARS (1977) *gives the moviegoer a vision of the new "air" adventures forthcoming in the cinema.*

The 1978 *SUPERMAN* was a far more convincing portrayal. Despite a languorous beginning, the script contained considerable humor and invention. Christopher Reeve, as the man from Krypton, performed with an appealing element of self-irony that is uncommon in the genre.

From a flying point of view, the film was miraculous. The technical tricks were of a high standard throughout, possibly the best on film. It was directed by the obviously gifted Richard Donner, who, despite the success of the film, quarrelled with the producers during the follow-up *SUPERMAN II* and was replaced by the talented Richard Lester. It is to be hoped that the "special effects" staff has been retained.

Aside from astronauts and cosmonauts and other space heroes, I hope that in the future somebody still feels like making films about flying and real flying adventures, perhaps from the period when it was still a time for heroes.

The veteran and famous stunt pilot Frank Tallman (Lt. Col. USMC Ret.) at his Fokker Triplane used in THE GREAT WALDO PEPPER (1975). *Tragically Tallman was killed in a crash during a reconnaissance trip in the mountains in 1978.*

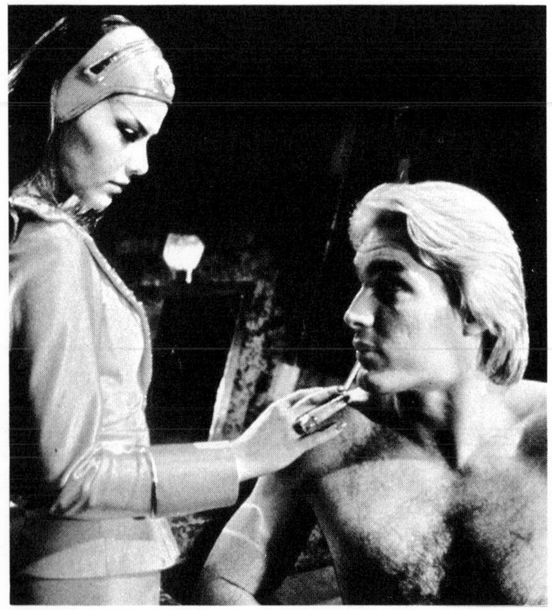

Sam Jones and Melody Anderson in FLASH GORDON (1980).

William A. Wellman–
A Director in Hollywood

"I made one of the best films in my life there. It was in 1956, but the movie public didn't agree. But the hell with them! It was GOODBYE, MY LADY *and it was a wonderful film, one of my best. I loved it. It was about a guy who had to give away his dog. That was all."*

A few years ago when I was first planning to write this book, I had an article from an American movie magazine fresh in my mind—an article that I was, alas, unable to trace. It was about the subject of flying films and had an interview with the veteran director William Wellman in which he said some things that I liked very much.

In many respects, Wellman is an unusual representative of the period of Hollywood's greatness, for better or for worse. He was an all-around director who worked within this tough commercial entertainment industry and retained his self-respect in most of the various film genres. Although his work was often uneven, there still remain a number of his films—against all odds—which carry his special stamp and convey some personal vitality. Especially as regards films about flying, Wellman represents a kind of symbol for me, and so I decided when I was traveling in America that I would try to meet him and possibly interview him for my book. Unfortunately, it was not in the stars. I traveled to the United States, but I was too late—William Wellman died of leukemia in 1975.

But since he greatly fascinated me and represented some sort of inspiration for this whole anthology, I thought I would try to tell something about his life as a filmmaker.

My information is based mainly on an interview he gave to Debra Weiner and Patrick McGilligan, translated by Johan Holmér and published in the Swedish magazine *Chaplin* in November 1976. In addition to some other sources I have also found important information in Richard Schickel's *The Men Who Made the Movies* (1975).

William A. Wellman

William Augustus Wellman was born in 1896 and grew up in a small town in Massachusetts. His childhood appears to have been filled with considerable problems—when speaking about it, Wellman joked very much about his boyhood but one has the impression that behind this joking there was really not much fun. At one time he was sentenced to six months on probation and his own mother was appointed his probation officer—after which he decided to leave home for good.

Some versions of this story maintain that he simply ran away. Whatever the case, he entered a new phase of life that was extremely chaotic. After a variety of temporary jobs—a kind of concentrated university of life—he was finally able to do what he had always dreamed of doing. He learned to fly.

To get training of this kind at the time—around 1915—was nearly impossible if one did not have a large fortune behind one. But there was one way. Millionaire William K. Vanderbilt had formed a volunteer flying corps as a means of sending aid to the French in the war in Europe. This corps was later named the "Lafayette Flying Corps" and a search was carried out for young men who wished to become pilots. The youthful William Wellman—he was 19 or 20—became one of these, and when he had completed his training he was shipped over to Europe along with other young men to take part in the air battles above the trenches.

His experience as a fighter pilot in Escadrille SPA 87 influenced him for the rest of his life. Time after time he returned to this experience—time after time he used it as a theme in his films about war. In certain statements he often made heroes out of his comrades, and one always has the feeling that this was how Wellman really saw them: he saw many of them die, he himself survived. He retained a strong loyalty to these memories and he praised these young men many times both in his films and in statements he made about them:

I'm proud of that time. I think we were the first American volunteers before the U.S. entered the war. We were volunteers and we made history, and I'm proud of it. Really proud.

In his youth Wellman was also a good ice hockey player. When he played a series of matches in Boston there was an important person among the spectators who took an interest in this tough young "pirate" (he was the fastest member of the team). This person was Douglas Fairbanks. He introduced himself to the young man and this was the beginning of a long friendship. One day the young fighter pilot on the Western Front received a telegram from Fairbanks: "When it's all over there will always be a job for you."

After the war, Wellman worked for a while as an instructor at a flying school, where he taught his student pilots the art of air battle. The flying school was in San Diego and Wellman often flew to Fairbanks' estate to visit the film star. He used to land his plane on the estate's own racetrack. It was at Fairbanks' place that he got to know most of the Hollywood stars of the time: Charlie Chaplin, Pola Negri, Harold Lloyd and Mary Pickford, to name only a few. And it was in this way that Wellman's own film career began. Fairbanks gave him a part in a film—*The Knickerbocker Buckaroo*. When the 23-year-old Wellman saw himself on the screen he was very disappointed. The following conversation between Wellman and Fairbanks was recalled in an interview by Debra Weiner and Patrick McGilligan:

A 20-year-old Bill Wellman was photographed in his aviator uniform.

"I've got nothing against acting, but I'm just no good at it," said Wellman.
"What do you want to be then?" Fairbanks asked.
"I want to be a director," he said.

And that is the way it was. Fairbanks introduced him to the Goldwyn Studios and he applied the same energy to making a career in films as he had in learning to fly—obviously Wellman devoted himself to these two activities with an intensity close to passion. Behind all the self-irony and disillusioned talk of life in Hollywood there remains still a real love for the medium of film. And Wellman learned the work from the ground up.

He started as a "go-for," prop-man and cutter's assistant, and then assistant director—to, among others, the action specialist

Bernie Durning—and finally he was given his first job as director. The film was called *The Man Who Won* (1923), and it was so successful that he was able to carry on making more. All his efforts were not so good by a long shot, but Wellman himself was always the first to admit it when he failed with something. He seldom bragged about his films although he was certainly proud when they were good:

"Whenever I am asked to give a talk I usually begin by saying that I've made some very bad films, and I think I'm fairly alone in admitting this. Wyler and Capra and all the others, even Jack Ford, only talk about their successes. Besides myself, Raoul Walsh is the only other one who doesn't. And I like him very much. We're very much alike, Walsh and I." He said this in the interview and he has made similar statements many times.

His self-criticism was real enough, but sometimes it sounds a little like praise in reverse. In his eagerness not to sound "special," not to play the "deeply serious" director, Wellman often overdoes it. There is something here in his character that could be described as typically American—the desire to appear just a tough, simple guy, to be a man of action, the fear of being regarded as an intellectual or "artist" who has a message to convey in his films or stories.

The same quality can be seen in Wellman's colleagues, John Ford and Howard Hawks—but most obvious perhaps in their literary "father": Hemingway. This slightly naive feature has both its good and bad sides, and when it comes to film the good aspects consist of a kind of fresh, original storytelling ability, straight and often wonderful simplicity . . .

Wellman's first big success was *You Never Know Women* (1926), and then came *WINGS* (1927), the film we mentioned earlier that brought him an Oscar for the best film of the year. The famous Oscar statuette was born in 1927 and *WINGS* was the first film, among stiff competition, to win the award.

Beggars of Life (1928) Wellman himself considered to be the best silent movie he made. After this he made one or two films every year, such productions as *Chinatown Nights* (1929), *The Man I Love* (1929), *The Public Enemy* (1931). The last mentioned was epoch-making in a sense and established a style in gangster films.

WINGS (1927)

In 1935 he made *Call of the Wild,* with Clark Gable and Jack Oakie in the leading roles as Jack Thornton and Shorty Hollihan. The following year he directed *Small Town Girl,* and also in 1936 *A Star Is Born* with Janet Gaynor and Fredric March. This bitter and revealing story about the dream factory's scrap heap was among the finest pictures Wellman made. Despite reports to the contrary, he himself wrote the story and supplied the tense direction. The story was later filmed in an honorable repeat with Judy Garland and James Mason (1954), but when another remake was done in the seventies with Barbra Streisand and Kris Kristofferson it was watered down to thin stuff indeed.

MEN WITH WINGS (1938) was one of Wellman's better flying stories, and one of the adventure stories most remembered from one's own youth was *Beau Geste,* with Wellman's favorite actor—Gary Cooper—in the lead. *Beau Geste* had a kind of naive charm, a sort of boys'-own freshness that is doubtless *passé* now, but is still memorable for anyone who experienced it in those impressionable years.

The most powerful of all Wellman's films was perhaps *The Ox-Bow Incident,* made in 1943. This was a frighteningly compelling story based on a novel by Walter Van Tilburg Clark; the screenplay was written by Lamar Trotti. In this film were Henry Fonda and Dana Andrews in beautifully drawn character roles, and a sensational Latin American type by the name of Anthony Quinn: for Quinn especially, this film represented a personal breakthrough in films.

Technically speaking, *The Ox-Bow Incident* was certainly not Wellman's greatest work—it had a low budget and he had to use leftover backdrops and shaky back projection—but artistically it was his masterpiece: it was a simple, straightforward fable which reached a large public (and indeed still does), a fable that cannot be misunderstood. The film is a poignant sermon against the evil of the lynching mentality.

Another story was *The Story of G.I. Joe* (1945). This was based on two books by the famous war correspondent Ernie Pyle: *Here Is Your War* and *Brave Men.* It had rather too much pathos and was greatly influenced by the times. But this film was among Wellman's own favorites and he says in the interview with Weiner and McGilligan:

I think it was the best film I made. I loved Ernie. One-hundred-and-fifty guys—and it's a tragic story. They worked for me and they went to the South Pacific. Ernie went with them, and none of them ever came back. The terrible thing is that I got to know all those guys, I began to like them. I gave them extra pay and everything, and then suddenly it was all over.

When the film *The Iron Curtain* was made in 1948, Wellman was accused of belonging to the extreme right. When he made *The Ox-Bow Incident,* he was accused of being a left-wing radical. The truth is that he was probably somewhere in the middle. The majority of Wellman's films are marked by a strong sense of justice and individualism—

From the shooting of MY MAN AND I (1952). It was called LETTER FROM THE PRESIDENT *at the beginning. Wellman is seen with Shelley Winters and Vittorio Gassman.*

but he was hardly a political analyst. In some of the statements he made in later years he was very noncommittal: he preferred to be regarded as a political idiot or wild maverick—and, again, the simple guy on the street who scorns all power and intrigues.

In 1954 William Wellman made *THE HIGH AND THE MIGHTY* together with his good friend, the writer Ernest K. Gann, which was a small masterpiece of sorts. By this time, he had over eighty films behind him. It was probably more but he himself lost count when some of the original negatives "disappeared" from the archives.

And then came the end, in 1957. It happened with a production called *C'EST LA GUERRE* and it had to do with a period that meant a lot to Wellman personally, about the Lafayette squadron. It was to be a film in praise of the comrades with whom he had fought in the First World War, comrades he had seen die. As we mentioned previously in the book, the film did not turn out the way Wellman wanted it to. Jack Warner, all-powerful producer, ruthlessly changed the story so that it was nothing but mush and finished with a happy end. And he also changed the title to *LAFAYETTE ESCADRILLE*.

These changes caused Wellman to see red. He had never liked Jack Warner—they had quarrelled in the thirties when Warner added a contrived ending to *Wild Boys of the Road* (1933), one of Wellman's socially committed films about serious youth problems. Things between them were not better now. Wellman walked out of the studio without actually completing the film—and after that he never made another movie. At the age of 62 he was finished with Hollywood and went into retirement.

Finally, I have chosen to end this note on William Wellman by allowing the man himself to sum up his life in films. The quotation is taken from a book he wrote, as related to Weiner and McGilligan in their interview with him:

Do I remember everything the way it was, the way it really was? No, I remember things as though they were seen from high up in the air, I see a stadium filled with people without recognizing their faces, or the way you remember a love affair without recalling who you shared it with. To the memory of those I have loved, those I have flown with. Some comes from them, some from myself, but they're all misty figures from my past, who I will never forget. I made my living by making films, by reading what fine writers were writing about, and on occasion transferring their works to film, to be seen and loved by millions of people. The words were beautiful, but lacked something that I had to give them: a performance, pictures, as the words themselves demanded. Every film director goes his own way, and I did it my way. This was the start of a personal style, which by being repeated took shape in hundreds of films, all with different content, played by hundreds of actors, men and women, and written together with hundreds of authors and screenwriters, I used much of their style, their humor, their sadness, their dialogue, but not always their ideas. Many of my writer friends, such as Gene Fowler and Ben Hecht, and the calm lovable Lamar Trotti, I saw as fantastic actors. They performed when they wrote. They gave me a style that is all my own, for better or for worse and more or less original, and they are a part of it.

A list of William Wellman's films follows. For reasons of space and the fact that the titles of those which have "disappeared" are not known, only the most important ones are named.

ISLAND IN THE SKY (1953). *From left: John Wayne, Hal Baylor, Wally Cassell and Robert Keys (?).*

Films of William A. Wellman

Original titles (premiere year)

The Man Who Won (1923)
Second-Hand Love (1923)
Big Dan (1923)
Cupid's Fireman (1923)
The Vagabond Trail (1924)
Not a Drum Was Heard (1924)
The Circus Cowboy (1924)
When Husbands Flirt (1925)
The Boob (1926)
The Cat's Pajamas (1926)
You Never Know Women (1926)
Wings (1927)
The Legion of the Condemned (1928)
Ladies of the Mob (1928)
Beggars of Life (1928)
Chinatown Nights (1929)
The Man I Love (1929)
Woman Trap (1929)
Dangerous Paradise (1930)
Young Eagles (1930)
Maybe It's Love (1930)
Other Men's Women (1931)
The Public Enemy (1931)
Night Nurse (1931)
Star Witness (1931)
Safe in Hell (1931)
The Hatchet Man (1932)
So Big (1932)
Love Is a Racket (1932)
The Purchase Price (1932)
The Conquerors (1932)
Frisco Jenny (1933)
Central Airport (1933)
Lilly Turner (1933)
Midnight Mary (1933)
Heroes for Sale (1933)
Wild Boys of the Road (1933)
College Coach (1933)
Looking for Trouble (1934)
Stingaree (1934)
The President Vanishes (1934)
Call of the Wild (1935)
The Robin Hood of El Dorado (1936)
Small Town Girl (1936)
A Star Is Born (1937)
Nothing Sacred (1937)
Men with Wings (1938)
Beau Geste (1939)
The Light that Failed (1939)
Reaching for the Sun (1941)
Roxie Hart (1942)
The Great Man's Lady (1942)
Thunder Birds (1942)
The Ox-Bow Incident (1943)
Lady of Burlesque (1943)
Buffalo Bill (1944)
This Man's Navy (1945)
The Story of G.I. Joe (1945)
Gallant Journey (1946)
Magic Town (1947)
The Iron Curtain (1948)
Yellow Sky (1949)
Battleground (1949)
The Happy Years (1950)
Across the Wild Missouri (1951)
Westward the Women (1952)
It's a Big Country (1952) Episode
My Man and I (1952)
Island in the Sky (1953)
The High and the Mighty (1954)
Track of the Cat (1954)
Blood Alley (1955)
Goodbye My Lady (1956)
Darby's Rangers (1958)
Lafayette Escadrille (1958)

Glenn Ford and Janet Blair have a chat with Bill Wellman during a break in GALLANT JOURNEY (1946).

Top Ten List

The author's personal list of the top ten films about flying with an additional ten films worth remembering.

1. THE DAWN PATROL (1938)
2. DIVE BOMBER (1941)
3. AIR FORCE (1943)
4. TWELVE O'CLOCK HIGH (1949)
5. THE SOUND BARRIER (1952)
6. WINGS (1927)
7. THE WAR LOVER (1962)
8. STRATEGIC AIR COMMAND (1955)
9. THE BRIDGES AT TOKO-RI (1954)
10. THE FIGHTING LADY (1944)
11. THE WAY TO THE STARS (1945)
12. ONLY ANGELS HAVE WINGS (1939)
13. THE MEMPHIS BELLE (1944)
14. THE FIRST OF THE FEW (1942)
15. TOWARD THE UNKNOWN (1956)
16. TARGET FOR TONIGHT (1941)
17. CAPTAINS OF THE CLOUDS (1942)
18. THE FIRST SQUADRON (1941)
19. THIRTY SECONDS OVER TOKYO (1944)
20. D 111 88 (1938)

Steve McQueen in THE WAR LOVER (1962).

Next two pages: A Spad XIII flying in William Wellman's MEN WITH WINGS (1938).

Acknowledgments

I would like to extend my warm gratitude to all the film companies and institutions and persons who have helped to make this film anthology possible.

Film Companies

Cinema International Corporation
Metro-Goldwyn-Mayer Inc.
Paramount Pictures Corporation
20th Century-Fox International Corporation
United Artists
Universal-International
Columbia-Warner

Institutions

Academy of Motion Pictures, Arts and Sciences, Hollywood, U.S.A.
Air Force Museum, Wright-Paterson AFB, Ohio, U.S.A.
1361st Audiovisual Squadron, AAVS (MAC), Arlington, U.S.A.
Eddie Brandt's Saturday Matinee, Hollywood, U.S.A.
Filmarchive/Deutsches Institute für Filmkunde, Wiesbaden, BRD/W.G.
Larry Edmund's Bookshop, Hollywood, U.S.A.
Swedish Air Force Air Support Squadron, F7, Sweden
Swedish Film Institute, Stockholm, Sweden

Persons

Carl-Gustaf Ahremark, Linköping, Sweden
George Bisset, Stockholm, Sweden
Bengt Börjesson, Sollentuna, Sweden
Jahn Charleville, Stockholm
Peter Cowie, London, England
Brenda Davies, British Film Institute, London
Kenne Fant, Swedish Film Industry, Stockholm
Glenn Ford, Hollywood, U.S.A.
Bengt Fredholm, Blentarp, Sweden
Gunnar Jansson, Linköping
Clyde Jeavons, National Film Archive, London
Sune Johansson, Linköping
Torsten Jungstedt, Stockholm
Alf Kjellin, Hollywood, U.S.A.
Leif Krantz, Stockholm
Aleksander Kwiatkowski, Swedish Film Institute, Stockholm
Gunnar Lindquist, Stockholm
Reinhold Nilsson, Nyköping, Sweden
Margareta Nordström, Swedish Film Institute, Stockholm
Olle Rosberg, Swedish Film Institute, Stockholm
Berit Skogsberg, Stockholm
Ingvar Skogsberg, Stockholm
Michelle Snapes, National Film Archive, London
Eberhard Spiess, Deutsches Institute für Filmkunde, Wiesbaden, West Germany
Leila Sturell, Warner-Columbia Film, Stockholm
Sven-Gunnar Särman, Höganäs, Sweden
Monica Tromm, Fox-Stockholm Film, Stockholm
Bertil Wredlund, Swedish Film Institute, Stockholm
Maj-Britt Zöhrer, CIC AB, Stockholm

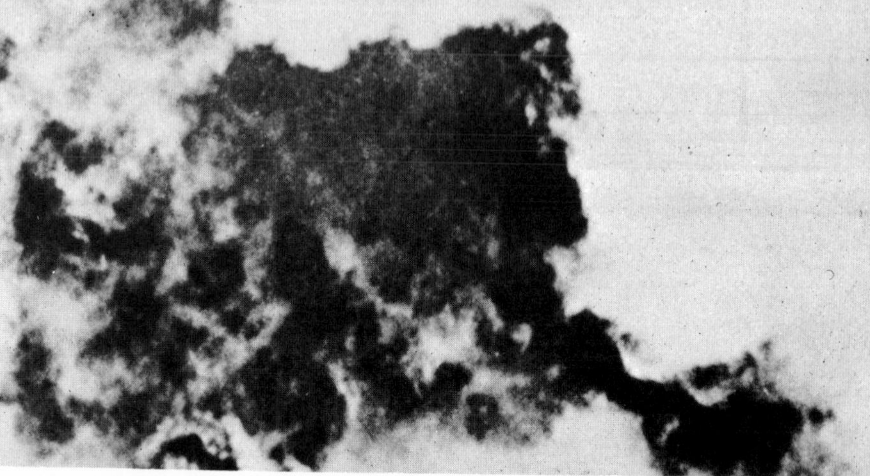

Bibliography

Amberg, George, ed. *New York Times Film Reviews.* New York: Quadrangle Books Inc., 1972.

American Film Institute Catalog of Motion Pictures. New York: R.R. Bowker Co.

Anderson, Joseph L., and Donald Ritchie. *The Japanese Film: Art and Industry.* New York: Grove Press Inc., 1960.

Ballantine's Illustrated History of World War II, Nos. 17 and 29. New York: Ballantine Books Inc.

Baxter, John. *Hollywood in the Thirties.* San Diego: A.S. Barnes, 1968.

Behlmer, Rudy. "World War I Aviation Films." *Films in Review,* August to October, 1967.

Dickens, Homer. *The Films of James Cagney.* New York: Citadel Press, 1972.

Deschner, Donald. *The Films of Cary Grant.* New York: Citadel Press, 1975.

Dimmitt, Richard B. *Title Guide to the Talkies.* Metuchen, New Jersey: Scarecrow Press Inc., 1965.

Essoe, Gabe. *The Films of Clark Gable.* New York: Citadel Press, 1970.

Guinness History of Air Warfare. Brown/Shores/ Macksey.

Halliwell, Leslie. *Filmgoer's Companion,* 2nd and 5th ed. New York: Avon Books.

International Motion Picture Almanac, 1935–1977. New York: Quigley Publishing Co.

Jablonski, Edward. *Flying Fortress.* Garden City, New York: Doubleday and Co., 1965.

Jeavons, Clyde. *A Pictorial History of War Films.* New York: Citadel Press, 1974.

Leiser, Erwin. *Nazi Cinema.* Riverside, New Jersey: MacMillian Co., 1975.

McCarty, Clifford, et al. *The Films of Errol Flynn.* New York, Citadel Press, 1971.

McCarty, Clifford. *Bogey: The Films of Humphrey Bogart.* New York: Citadel Press, 1970.

Manvell, Roger, and Lewis Jacob, eds. *The International Film Encyclopedia.* New York: Crown, 1972.

Michael, Paul. *American Movies Reference Book.* Englewood, New Jersey: Prentice-Hall Inc., 1968.

Morella, Joe, et al. *The Films of World War II.* New York: Citadel Press, 1973.

Ricci, Mark, et al. *The Films of John Wayne.* New York: Citadel Press, 1972.

Robinson, David. *Hollywood in the Twenties.* San Diego: A.S. Barnes, 1968.

Schickel, Richard. *The Men Who Made the Movies.* New York: Atheneum, 1975.

Thomas, Tony. *Films of the Forties.* New York: Citadel Press, 1977.

Weaver, John T. *Forty Years of Screen Credits, 1929–1969.* Metuchen, New Jersey: Scarecrow Press Inc., 1970.

Weiner, Debra and Patrick McGilligan. "Alla djävla sorters filmer." *Chaplin,* November, 1976.

Willis, John, ed. *Screen World 1949–1976.* New York: Crown Publishers Inc.

Winshester, Clarence, ed. *World Film Encyclopedia.* New York: Gordon Press, 1933.

Other general sources: *Chaplin,* Stockholm: 1965–1976; *Filmrutan,* Stockholm: 1969–1976; *Picturegoer 1932,* July to December; *Säsongens Filmer,* 1928–1974.

Tyrone Power as a young pilot in A YANK IN THE R.A.F. (1941).

Indexes

Films

- *English translations of foreign film titles appear in italics.*
- *Title changes for American or British markets appear in boldface.*
- *Italic numerals indicate a photograph.*
- *Foreign films are also listed by nation following this index.*

Helen Hayes and Clark Gable in the very romantic THE WHITE SISTER (1933).

William Gargan, at right, with Kent Taylor in THE SKY PARADE (1936).

Bud Abbott and Lou Costello are "on top of the world" in KEEP 'EM FLYING (1940).

James Donald and Noel Willman in THE NET (1953).

LUFTENS VAGABOND

EN SVENSK FILM I NY STIL MED
KAPTEN ALBIN AHRENBERG

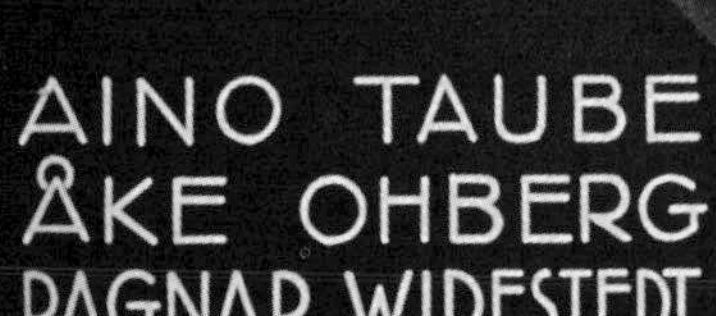

REGI:
WEYLER HILDEBRAND

PRODUKTION:
AERO-FILM

ENSAMRÄTT: A-B. EUROPA-FILM

Foreign Films

Poster for the Swedish film LUFTENS VAGABOND (1933) (The Vagabond of the Air).

Victor deKowa in DES TEUFELS GENERAL (1955).

Actors, Directors, Authors and Others

Italic numerals indicate a photograph.

Robert Wagner after he has parachuted in THE HUNTERS (1958).

1046-46

Aircraft

Aircraft

Aircraft in the book have been identified to the best of the author's ability. Italics indicate a photograph.

Myrna Loy as the tough and loveable woman pilot in James Flood's WINGS IN THE DARK (1935). *The plane is a Seversky EP-1.*

George Formby in IT'S IN THE AIR (1938). *The plane is a Hawker Hart.*